353·031309

D0480984

A2 Gove.   at & Politics

The Presidency & Presidential Power

Anthony J. Bennett

Advanced TopicMaster

2nd Edition

Series editor
Eric Magee

2 2 MAR 2010

10069819

Philip Allan Updates, an imprint of Hodder Education, an Hachette UK company, Market Place, Deddington, Oxfordshire OX15 0SE

Orders

Bookpoint Ltd, 130 Milton Park, Abingdon, Oxfordshire, OX14 4SB
tel: 01235 827720
fax: 01235 400454
e-mail: uk.orders@bookpoint.co.uk
Lines are open 9.00 a.m.–5.00 p.m., Monday to Saturday, with a 24-hour message answering service. You can also order through the Philip Allan Updates website: www.philipallan.co.uk

© Philip Allan Updates 2010

ISBN 978-1-4441-0779-1

Printed in Spain

Hachette UK's policy is to use papers that are natural, renewable and recyclable products and made from wood grown in sustainable forests. The logging and manufacturing processes are expected to conform to the environmental regulations of the country of origin.

Contents

Introduction

The growth in the office of the presidency

If you want to see how the office of the US presidency has evolved from relative unimportance to great significance, try to name the US presidents before 1933: that is, before Franklin D. Roosevelt. Thirty men held the office between 1789 and 1932. I should be surprised if you could name even six of them. I should be even more surprised if your list included John Tyler (1841–45), Millard Fillmore (1850–53), Franklin Pierce (1853–57) or Rutherford Hayes (1877–81). The point is simply this: until the 1930s the federal government as a whole was neither particularly large nor particularly relevant to Americans in their everyday lives. Most government at that time was being done by the state governments rather than by the federal government. It wasn't until the introduction of the New Deal by Franklin D. Roosevelt (FDR) in the 1930s and the beginning of the USA's role as a world power in the 1940s that the federal government became important in the lives of ordinary Americans. As the role of the federal government became more important, almost inevitably the role of the presidency increased. Now see how many you can name of the 12 men who have held the office of president from FDR (1945) to the present day. You might well get all of them.

The paradoxes of the office of the presidency

Significance and notoriety are not synonymous with power. What we will pursue here is what Thomas Cronin and Michael Genovese call, in the title of their 1998 book, *The Paradoxes of the American Presidency* (Oxford University Press). 'Paradox' is the term we use for two seemingly contradictory things. According to Cronin and Genovese, the US presidency is characterised by nine paradoxes:

- Americans demand powerful leadership but they are suspicious of strong leadership and the abuse of power.
- The president is expected to be a 'common person' but to exhibit uncommon charisma, vision and leadership.
- The president is expected to be compassionate and decent but to be ruthless and cunning.
- Americans admire bipartisanship and think the president should to some extent be 'above politics', yet the presidency is the most political office in the US system of government.

- Americans want a president who will unite diverse peoples and interests, but presidents must make tough, unpopular decisions that will inevitably be divisive.
- Presidents are expected to have a visionary programme but still be pragmatic: they must be both leaders and followers.
- Presidents must be supremely self-confident but not portray themselves as infallible or above criticism.
- What it takes to become president may not be what is needed to govern the nation.
- The presidency is sometimes too strong, yet at other times too weak.

What Cronin and Genovese conclude is this: 'To govern successfully, a president must manage these paradoxes and must balance a variety of competing demands and expectations.' This makes the presidency a tricky office in which to succeed. And that's before we remember all those checks that exist on the presidency, which make the job even more difficult.

The checks on the office of the presidency

When the Founding Fathers wrote the Constitution in 1787, they were determined to check the power of the single chief executive they had created. They feared tyranny — the kind of unchecked executive power they had experienced under British colonial rule in the years before the War of Independence. So they hedged the president about with all kinds of checks, mostly by Congress: the president's vetoes can be overridden by a two-thirds majority in both houses of Congress; many of the president's executive and all of the judicial appointments must be approved by the Senate; treaties that the president negotiates must be confirmed by a two-thirds majority vote in the Senate; Congress can investigate, impeach, try and remove from office not only the president but any executive branch member. The Supreme Court, meanwhile, can declare the laws that the president has signed and the actions the president takes to be unconstitutional. And that's not a comprehensive list.

One must then add into the formula the fact that the president's party may not necessarily be the majority party in one or either house of Congress. Members of the House and Senate do not feel that their political futures are necessarily tied up with the success or failure of the president. The president is physically separate from Congress, as is the cabinet. All this makes the presidency a limited and checked office.

This brings us back to Cronin and Genovese and their ninth paradox: the presidency is sometimes too strong and sometimes too weak. Sometimes a number of factors combine to make the presidency powerful. Here are three such factors:

- The president is usually stronger if recently elected — or re-elected — with a large majority of the popular vote. In 1932, FDR was elected with 57% of the popular vote, which gave him an 18 percentage point winning margin over his Republican opponent, Herbert Hoover. Similarly, in 1984, Ronald Reagan was re-elected with 59% of the popular vote and an 18 percentage point margin over his Democrat opponent, Walter Mondale.
- At a time of crisis, the presidency usually becomes more powerful, especially when that crisis is associated with a threat to the nation's security. Thus, FDR during the Second World War, John F. Kennedy at the time of the Cuban missile Crisis and George W. Bush after 11 September 2001 benefited from presiding over a more powerful office.
- When one party controls both the White House and both houses of Congress, this can enhance the power of the presidency: Lyndon Johnson (1965–66) is a good example.

If these and other factors coincide, the constitutional checks and balances impinge less on the presidency, making the president's programme and policies more doable. It would be highly unusual for a president who had the benefit of even two of the factors mentioned above to have presidential vetoes overridden, appointments blocked or treaties rejected, or to be impeached. There is some reason to believe that the checks and balances of the Constitution work better when, for example, the president and the majority of both houses of Congress are of different parties.

At the time of writing (mid-2009), the last time Congress overrode a presidential veto was in 2008, when a Democrat-controlled Congress overrode a veto from Republican George W. Bush. The last time a cabinet appointment was rejected by the Senate was in 1989, when a Democrat-controlled Senate rejected a nomination from Republican George H. W. Bush. The last time a treaty was rejected by the Senate was in 1999, when a Republican-controlled Senate rejected a treaty negotiated by Democrat Bill Clinton. And the only times in recent history when impeachment proceedings began in Congress were in 1974, when the Democrat-controlled Congress drew up articles of impeachment against Republican president Richard Nixon, and then in 1998, when the Republican-controlled Congress impeached Democrat president Bill Clinton on two counts.

That's not to say that a president whose party controls both houses of Congress does not feel the effects of congressional checks and balances — ask Jimmy Carter about energy legislation, Bill Clinton about healthcare reform or

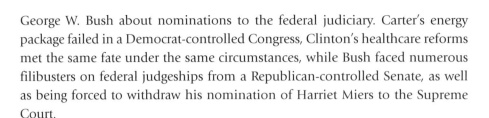

George W. Bush about nominations to the federal judiciary. Carter's energy package failed in a Democrat-controlled Congress, Clinton's healthcare reforms met the same fate under the same circumstances, while Bush faced numerous filibusters on federal judgeships from a Republican-controlled Senate, as well as being forced to withdraw his nomination of Harriet Miers to the Supreme Court.

Changes in the office of the presidency

The presidency is an ever-changing institution. First, the presidency has changed as a result of such constitutional changes as the two-term limit (22nd Amendment) introduced in 1951. As a consequence, Dwight Eisenhower, Ronald Reagan, Bill Clinton and George W. Bush could not run again for office in 1960, 1988, 2000 and 2008 respectively. Admittedly, it seems unlikely that Eisenhower, Reagan or probably Bush would have run for a third term even had the 22nd Amendment not been in place. Reagan, for example, was just a month shy of his 78th birthday when he left office in January 1989. But Clinton is quite a different matter. He was only in his mid-50s when he left office after two terms in January 2001. And although he had low approval ratings, he was still personally popular and an impressive electioneer.

Second, the presidency has changed as a result of changes elsewhere in US politics. Significant reforms to the process for choosing presidential candidates have changed the presidency. It is now much more likely that the candidate will be a Washington outsider with few links with Congress — men like Jimmy Carter, Bill Clinton or George W. Bush. This has implications for governing. Congress has become a place in which power is more diffuse than it was in the 1950s or 1960s. No longer can presidents deal with just a few powerful party leaders and committee chairs. They have to deal with 535 individual members. The growth in the size and scope of the federal government has led to the formation of the Executive Office of the President and the growth in the number of executive departments from the original three in 1789 to the current 15.

Third, the presidency has changed as a result of crises: Vietnam, Watergate, the Iran–Contra scandal, Bill Clinton's impeachment and 9/11 have all left their mark on the presidency. Vietnam and Watergate fostered distrust of the presidency as well as some institutional reforms that changed the presidency — reforms such as the War Powers Act (1973), which limited the president's manoeuvrability in using troops abroad. Clinton's impeachment further tarnished the presidential office and increased scepticism. The events of 11 September 2001 led to an increase in presidential power, as so often occurs at times when national security is thought to be on the line.

Finally, the presidency has changed as a result of the 43 individuals who have occupied the presidential office. Their personalities have left a mark: Nixon's suspicions, Reagan's optimism, Clinton's perjury, George W. Bush's swagger and Obama's energy. The office would probably have been quite different if their one-time opponents — Hubert Humphrey, Walter Mondale, Bob Dole, Al Gore and John McCain — had become president.

The difficulties in the office of the presidency

Many of the changes that have swept through the presidency have made it a more difficult office in which to succeed, as the following extract shows:

> 'Any job', writes management expert Peter Drucker, 'that has defeated two or three men in succession, even though each had performed well in his previous assignments, must be assumed unfit for human beings. It must be redesigned.' By this measure, the American presidency is both a troubled and troubling institution. Something is wrong. Once seen as the great engine of American democracy, the presidency now seems to be 'the little train that can't!' Where have all the leaders gone?
>
> From the heady days of presidential power in the 1930s, when Franklin D. Roosevelt was both powerful and purposeful, we now face a system that is characterised by gridlock and deadlock, paralysis and roadblocks. From Lyndon Johnson to Bill Clinton, recent presidents have either failed or performed well below expectations. The recent presidents have been unable to provide America with the leadership necessary to fulfil the Constitution's pledge to 'form a more perfect union, establish justice, ensure domestic tranquillity, provide for the common defence and general welfare, and secure the blessings of liberty'.
>
> As Phil Williams noted: 'The history of the American presidency since the early 1960s is one of failure.' Presidential scholar Thomas E. Cronin reminds us that 'presidential frustration is far more the rule than presidential triumph'.
>
> When between 1976 and 1992, three of four incumbent presidents lost their bids for re-election and all of the last seven presidents have left the office under less-than-desirable circumstances, it should be obvious that something is wrong. Yet when one enquires into the source(s) of these repeated failures, the explanation is usually: blame the person not the institution.
>
> Michael A. Genovese, 'The limits of presidential power', in W. F. Grover
and J. G. Pescheck (2006) Voices of Dissent, Longman

Obama has a more difficult job in being president than John F. Kennedy, nearly 40 years earlier. On entering the Oval Office, Obama had little Washington experience. The national party had not really chosen him as they had chosen JFK almost four decades earlier. Obama had been chosen in the primaries by the party's grassroots, not by the party bosses of Kennedy's era. And

Congress is far less biddable than when either Kennedy or Lyndon Johnson was president back in the 1960s.

The federal government that Obama has to manage is much bigger than it had been under Kennedy. Six more executive departments have been created in the intervening years: Housing and Urban Development (1965); Transportation (1966); Energy (1977); Education (1979); Veterans' Affairs (1989); and Homeland Security (2002). Kennedy had only nine such departments to oversee; Obama has 15.

Obama holds an office that is weaker because it has been tarnished by the goings-on of Johnson over Vietnam, Nixon over Watergate and Reagan over Iran–Contra. Clinton's sexual indiscipline and verbal acrobatics did little to burnish the image of the presidency in the minds of most Americans. Neither did George W. Bush's unpopular war in Iraq. Here's how Patrick Caddell, an aide to Jimmy Carter, put it some 30 years ago:

> I think that when Kennedy was president, the president was given the assumption of being right. That has totally disappeared. Kennedy would find a press corps that was at least willing to give him the benefit of the doubt. There is no sense in avoiding the fact that Vietnam and particularly Watergate did enormous damage to the office of the presidency in terms of its power, particularly with other institutions.

In the 25 years between 1974 and 1999, Congress forced one president to resign and impeached another. This significantly weakened the institution of the presidency. George W. Bush came to the presidency in January 2001 determined 'to restore dignity to the Oval Office'. But more than just dignity, Bush wanted to restore power to the office — and the events of 11 September 2001 gave him a reason to do so. Alexander Hamilton, writing in *The Federalist* No. 70, had stated that in his view, 'energy in the executive is a leading character[istic] of government'. Americans are usually prepared to accept an 'energetic' presidency when the nation is facing a threat from outside. But as President Johnson discovered in the 1960s, presidential power and effectiveness can quickly evaporate if a significant and vocal proportion of the US people determines that the president has overplayed his hand to little effect.

The questions to be answered

The aim of this book is to discuss the key questions that people ask these days about the US presidency. First, *what does anyone need to become president?* This takes us back to the basic point that perhaps the root cause of problems regarding the presidency is the process by which candidates are nowadays chosen and then elected to the office.

From election we turn to issues of governing and consider some key questions regarding the institution itself and the way Oval Office occupants use it. So our second question is: *why do presidents bother with the cabinet?* Is this an over-rated institution that ought to have been forgotten long ago, or an under-used institution that could offer real help to beleaguered presidents?

The ability to deal with Congress is key to presidential effectiveness and this is the focus of our third question: *how can presidents win in Congress?* Fourth, we consider those adjectives that analysts have attached to the office for decades: 'imperial', 'imperilled', 'impotent'. So, *what happened to the imperial presidency?*

We then focus on the profound changes in the presidency over the past four decades. If President Kennedy were to return to Washington DC today, what would he recognise about the presidential office that he so suddenly vacated over four decades ago, and, more particularly, what would surprise him? *What has changed in the presidency since the 1960s?* This leads us on to the question: *how successful a president was George W. Bush?* Finally, we broaden out to ask: *what makes a good president?*

Throughout the book, you may find many surprises. The US presidency is quite unlike the institution casual observers perceive it to be. It is often less powerful, more frustrating, less attractive and more limited than first meets the eye. So many people want to *become* president, but so few people, it seems, can *do* it.

To allow you to extend your research, further reading lists are given at the end of each chapter. Useful websites are as follows:

The presidency:

www.whitehouse.gov

www.presidency.ucsb.edu

www.americanpresident.org

www.clintonlibrary.gov

www.georgewbushlibrary.gov

Congress:

www.house.gov

www.senate.gov

www.c-span.org

www.centeroncongress.org

www.cqpolitics.com

What does anyone need to become president?

Some cynics might argue that possible short answers to this question could range from 'nothing much', through to 'be a good liar', to 'a great deal of money'. But I trust that you will consider all three answers to be both as shallow and inaccurate as they are brief. 'What does anyone need to become president?' is a question well worth asking. It might help us identify those criteria which, if possessed by a potential candidate, might lead him — or surely, one day, her — to be an effective president, and this is a question to which we shall return at the end of this book.

Constitutional requirements

First of all, let's clear the decks of the obvious answer to the question — that you must fulfil the requirements laid down in Article II of the Constitution. These are threefold: to be a natural-born US citizen; to be at least 35 years old; and to have been resident in the USA for at least 14 years. Since 1951, one could also add the requirement of the 22nd Amendment that one must not have already served two terms as president. Let us briefly consider these four 'needs'.

The requirement to be a natural-born US citizen is stricter than the citizenship requirement for a member of Congress. To be elected to Congress, one needs to be simply a US citizen, not a 'natural-born' US citizen. So, the Governor of California, Arnold Schwarzenegger, could be elected to the House of Representatives or the Senate, but not to the presidency. He is not a natural-born US citizen.

The age qualification may be the most surprising of all the requirements; not the age itself — 35 — but that there is an age qualification at all. Theodore Roosevelt (1901–09) stands as the youngest president. He was just 42 when he succeeded to the presidency following the assassination of William McKinley. John Kennedy (1961–63) stands as the youngest *elected* president. He was 43.

The residency qualification is a slight curiosity. It seems unlikely that anyone who had spent large portions of their adult life outside the USA would even be nominated as a presidential candidate.

The two-term limit was introduced in 1951 following Franklin D. Roosevelt's presidency of just over three complete terms. First elected in 1932, he was re-elected in 1936, 1940 and 1944, dying just 3 months into his fourth term of office. Many regarded George Washington's refusal to serve a third term in 1796 to be a convention that was well worth honouring. Republicans were particularly aggrieved (Roosevelt was a Democrat). In 1940, they had produced election badges that read: 'We don't want King Franklin the First' (some went further, adding: 'And we don't want Queen Eleanor either' — a less-than-subtle reference to the First Lady, Eleanor Roosevelt). To many Americans, a third — let alone a fourth — term smacked of the hereditary monarchies of old Europe. Hence the two-term amendment was passed in 1951. The four presidents directly affected by this amendment were Dwight Eisenhower (1953–61), Ronald Reagan (1981–89), Bill Clinton (1993–2001) and George W. Bush (2001–09). Eisenhower and Reagan were uninterested in a third term: Reagan was already 77 when he left office. The case of Bill Clinton, however, is quite different. And what of George W. Bush?

Extra-constitutional requirements

Having cleared the decks of the less interesting material, let's now address the question in another way. So far we have discovered what is absolutely essential. Now let's consider what would be helpful: those 'requirements' that are presumed rather than stated. We will call them 'extra-constitutional' requirements, as they are outside the Constitution. They are: political experience; major party endorsement; personal characteristics; the ability to raise large sums of money; effective organisation; oratorical skills and being telegenic; and sound, relevant policies.

Political experience

Conventional wisdom would tell us that if you want to become president of the USA, you need some significant political experience — and that really needs to be experience in an elective, rather than an appointed, office. Dwight Eisenhower, who was president between 1953 and 1961 and had never before

Condoleezza Rice

held elective office, is an obvious exception. But that occurred over 50 years ago and under unusual circumstances. This is not to say that there haven't been those who thought they might have followed in Eisenhower's footsteps. The name of General Colin Powell in the 1990s comes to mind, and even today some talk up the name of former Bush national security advisor and secretary of state, Condoleezza Rice. General Wesley Clarke ran for the Democratic presidential nomination in 2004 — but his candidacy quickly crashed. However, when presented in 2008 with the choice between two senators, one with less than 4 years of service in the Senate, the other with over 20 years, American voters chose the former — Barack Obama — over the latter, John McCain.

The particular types of political experience one needs to become president are senator, state governor or vice-president — or any combination of them (see Table 1.1). During the 1960s and 1970s, US senators seemed to be in favour — John Kennedy, Lyndon Johnson and Richard Nixon had all been in the Senate. Later, state governors were the favourites— Jimmy Carter, Ronald Reagan, Bill Clinton and George W. Bush had all been state governors. Even the list of presidential candidates seems to be drawn from these pools of recruitment. In 2008, the Democratic candidates for the presidency included four senators, two ex-senators and a state governor.

Until 2008, there had been a trend away from the president coming from Congress towards the president coming from among the state governors. Forty-three people have held the presidential office. Of the first 21 — George Washington (1789–97) to Chester Arthur (1881–85) — 16 had been in Congress. Of the last 22 — Grover Cleveland to Barack Obama — only ten had served in Congress; but that still makes 26 out of 43 presidents drawn from Congress.

During the last few decades, the vice-presidency has been regarded as a potential stepping stone to the presidency. Since 1960, two vice-presidents have stepped straight into the Oval Office without election — Vice-President Johnson on the death of President Kennedy in 1963, and Vice-President Ford on the resignation of President Nixon in 1974. Of the 12 vice-presidents since 1953, seven have gone on to be either the presidential candidate of their party or president. Richard Nixon, Lyndon Johnson, Gerald Ford and George H. W. Bush all became president, while Hubert Humphrey, Walter Mondale and Al Gore all became the Democratic presidential nominee. Of the remaining five, only one — Spiro Agnew — appears never to have aspired to presidential office.

Table 1.1 Public offices held before becoming president, 1961–2009

Date	President	Public office(s) held before becoming president
1961	John Kennedy	House of Representatives, senator
1963	Lyndon Johnson	House of Representatives, senator, vice-president
1969	Richard Nixon	House of Representatives, senator, vice-president
1974	Gerald Ford	House of Representatives, vice-president
1977	Jimmy Carter	State governor
1981	Ronald Reagan	State governor
1989	George H. W. Bush	House of Representatives, Republican National Committee chairman, CIA director, vice-president
1993	Bill Clinton	State governor
2001	George W. Bush	State governor
2009	Barack Obama	Senator

The House of Representatives has a poor record as a direct stepping-stone to the presidency — a further way in which it may be seen as a less prestigious house than the Senate. In 2008, the three House members running for their party's presidential nomination — Republicans Duncan Hunter and Ron Paul, as well as Democrat Dennis Kucinich — never looked liked winning even a primary, let alone the nomination. The last serving House member to be elected president was James Garfield in 1880! Within 4 months of being sworn in as president, Garfield was shot at Washington's Union Station while boarding a train to New Jersey. He died of his wounds 2 months later — not a good omen for members of the House of Representatives with presidential aspirations.

Why, between 1976 and 2004, did the best training for the presidency come to be seen as being a state governor rather than congressional experience? Four reasons may be worth considering:

● These three decades were characterised by an anti-Washington sentiment among the electorate. Those who ran for the presidency from a seat in Congress — Bob Dole for the Republicans in 1996 and John Kerry for the Democrats in 2004, for example — found it difficult to stop voters seeing them as out-of-touch, Washington politicians. Washington itself has its own

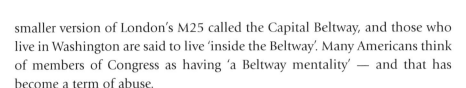

smaller version of London's M25 called the Capital Beltway, and those who live in Washington are said to live 'inside the Beltway'. Many Americans think of members of Congress as having 'a Beltway mentality' — and that has become a term of abuse.

- The states were seen as being more important than they used to be. The governor of a large state — Reagan of California or Bush of Texas — was regarded as a mini-president.
- This leads to a third reason: many opinion-makers regarded executive experience — as a state governor — as a better training ground to be chief executive (i.e. president) than legislative experience. Legislators talk; executives do.
- Finally, between 1989 and 2001 foreign policy receded as an important issue in presidential elections.

Major party endorsement

If you are going to make it to the White House, you need to be the presidential candidate of either the Republican or Democratic Party. To run as an independent or third-party candidate is not going to lead to your election. Strictly speaking, it is true to say that only major-party candidates have won the presidency. During the past century, in only a handful of elections did candidates not from major parties ever raise a serious challenge — 1912, 1948, 1968 and 1992 (see Table 1.2). In only one of these elections did the third-party candidate beat one of the major-party candidates. In 1912, former president Teddy Roosevelt came in second with 27.4% of the popular vote and 88 electoral college votes, while the Republican Party candidate and incumbent president William Howard Taft received just 23.2% of the popular vote and only 8 electoral college votes.

Table 1.2 Third-party and independent presidential candidates gaining more than 10% of the popular vote since 1912

Year	Third-party/independent candidate	Affiliation	Percentage of popular vote
1912	Theodore Roosevelt	Progressive Party	27.4
1924	Robert La Follette	Progressive Party	16.6
1968	George Wallace	American Independent Party	13.5
1992	Ross Perot	Independent	18.9

Even non-politicians such as Generals Dwight Eisenhower, Colin Powell and Wesley Clarke feel obliged to join a major party in order to be taken seriously as a presidential candidate. Third-party candidates generally struggle to get into single figures in terms of the percentage of the popular vote, let alone double figures. In the 2000 election, Green Party candidate Ralph Nader may well have played a decisive part in depriving Democrat Al Gore of Florida but he won less than 3% of the nationwide popular vote. The USA's two major parties are, in this sense, something of a paradox: although generally decentralised, undisciplined and of limited importance, they dominate all US elections — congressional as well as presidential.

Personal characteristics

Until 2008, all major party presidential candidates had been white males. One of the strongest women candidates of recent presidential elections —

Republican Elizabeth Dole in 2000 — pulled out of the race even before the first primaries and caucuses had got under way. Dole — a former Reagan and Bush cabinet officer and president of the American Red Cross — announced her departure from the race on 20 October 1999, a full 3 months before the Iowa caucuses. Former Democrat senator Carol Moseley Braun, an African-American, fared little better in her presidential bid in 2004. But then in 2008, former first lady and New York senator Hillary Clinton finished a strong second in the Democratic presidential primaries. Indeed, she had been expected to win the nomination before being beaten by an African-American, Barack Obama.

Hillary Clinton

Until Obama's nomination, the nearest an African-American had come to the presidential nomination of their party was the Reverend Jesse Jackson, who gained the second highest proportion of votes (29%) in the 1988 Democratic Party primaries — winning contests in Alabama, Georgia, Louisiana, Mississippi, Virginia, Michigan and Washington DC. At that year's Democratic National Convention, Jackson won 1,218 votes on the first ballot, but he was nowhere near the 2,876 votes secured by the eventual nominee, Governor Michael Dukakis of Massachusetts. In 2008, Obama won the Democratic presidential nomination — the first African-American to do so.

Table 1.3 Female senators, 2009

Name	Party	State
Lisa Murkowski	Republican	Alaska
Blanche Lincoln	Democrat	Arkansas
Barbara Boxer	Democrat	California
Dianne Feinstein	Democrat	California
Mary Landrieu	Democrat	Louisiana
Susan Collins	Republican	Maine
Olympia Snowe	Republican	Maine
Barbara Mikulski	Democrat	Maryland
Debbie Stabenow	Democrat	Michigan
Amy Klobuchar	Democrat	Minnesota
Claire McCaskill	Democrat	Missouri
Jeanne Shaheen	Democrat	New Hampshire
Kirsten Gillibrand	Democrat	New York
Kay Hagen	Democrat	North Carolina
Kay Bailey Hutchison	Republican	Texas
Patty Murray	Democrat	Washington
Maria Cantwell	Democrat	Washington

Table 1.4 Female state governors, 2009

Name	Party	State
Jan Brewer	Republican	Arizona
Jodi Rell	Republican	Connecticut
Linda Lingle	Republican	Hawaii
Jennifer Granholm	Democrat	Michigan
Christine Gregoire	Democrat	Washington

That there had been no serious female or black presidential candidates until 2008 was traceable to the fact that there were — and still are — very few female or black politicians in the two main pools of presidential recruitment: the US Senate and state governorships. Following the 2008 election cycle, just 17 of the 100 senators were women (see Table 1.3) and only one was black. As recently as 1990, there were only two female and no black senators. Among state governors in 2009 only five were women (see Table 1.4) and only one was governor of one of the largest states in terms of population — Jennifer Granholm of Michigan.

It is an advantage to be married. Of the 43 men who have held the presidency, only one — James Buchanan (1857–61) — was a bachelor. He was also one of only three presidents who did not have any children. Divorce, however, is no longer a barrier. Ronald Reagan divorced his first wife, Jane Wyman, in 1948, although that was 32 years before he was elected president, by which time he had been married to his second wife, Nancy, for 28 years.

There are mixed signals as to whether scandal is a bar to the presidency. The late Senator Edward Kennedy was never able to throw off the scandal surrounding the drowning of a young female acquaintance in his car after a late-night party in 1969. Senator Gary Hart pulled out of the 1988 nomination race after the press revealed photographs of the married senator with a scantily clad model, Donna Rice, on a yacht with the unfortunate name of *Monkey Business*. 'I'm not running for sainthood', protested Senator Hart. Soon he wasn't running for anything, forced from the race by a media firestorm. However, during the 1992 presidential primaries, Bill Clinton managed to survive allegations concerning a possible extra-marital relationship with Gennifer Flowers.

Ability to raise large sums of money

One of the many criticisms of US presidential elections is their expense. Many still think that you have to be personally rich to run for the presidency, but this is no longer the case. Indeed, personal wealth can become an embarrassment, as John Kerry discovered in 2004. Senator Kerry was said to be the richest person in the US Senate following his marriage to Teresa Heinz, the heiress to the Heinz business. A joke at Kerry's expense during the campaign was that he had just discovered the shortest and most successful fund-raising speech — 'I do'! Back in 1988, George H. W. Bush — born into a wealthy family — was ribbed by the governor of Texas, Ann Richards, as having been born 'with a silver foot in his mouth'. Richard Nixon, Gerald Ford, Jimmy Carter, Ronald Reagan, Bill Clinton and Barack Obama, however, had one thing in common — they were all born into poor families. Even by the time Obama became president, he was certainly not a wealthy person.

What you need to be able to do is to *raise* large sums of money. Just running for the presidential nomination of a major party is a hugely expensive business. In 2008, Hillary Clinton spent over $214 million losing in the Democratic primaries to Barack Obama. The same year, Mitt Romney spent over $100 million in his failed bid for the Republican nomination. Obama raised over $150 million in September 2008 alone. In 2008, Obama and McCain spent a

combined total of over $1 billion in their presidential races, with Obama spending well over twice as much as McCain — $711 million to McCain's $296 million. This gave Obama a huge advantage in the general election campaign.

Although personal wealth is no longer as important as it used to be in presidential politics, some high-profile and wealthy people have financed their own campaigns — notably Ross Perot in 1992, and Steve Forbes in 1996 and 2000.

Effective organisation

In a country as large as the USA and in a campaign as long as that for the presidency, effective organisation is imperative. There is a high degree of correlation between the best-organised campaign and the winning one. Writing in the *National Journal* (6 November 2004), commentator Charlie Cook stated:

> In a really competitive race, there is rarely one reason for a victory. But an important factor in President Bush's triumph surely is that the Bush–Cheney re-election effort was perhaps the best planned, best executed, most disciplined, and most strategic presidential campaign in history. The Bush campaign was exceptionally good. And it made very few mistakes.

Effective organisation can be vital in close elections by making a critical difference to turnout. In 2004, the Bush campaign put a huge effort into a 'Get out the vote' (GOTV) operation. After the 2000 election, Bush's political strategist Karl Rove set about trying to identify what he called 'the missing voters' — natural Bush supporters who did not show up on election day. Under Rove's direction, the Bush campaign launched a huge voter registration drive in those districts where Bush had underperformed in 2000. This GOTV scheme was test-run — successfully — at the 2002 midterm elections and then perfected in the 2004 presidential race. As a result, whereas high turnouts usually benefit the Democrats, in 2004 high turnout benefited the Republicans. Bush's victory in 2004 was significantly helped by effective organisation, just as poor organisation hindered the campaigns of Michael Dukakis (1988), Bob Dole (1996) and Al Gore (2000). In 2008, the Obama campaign was characterised by effectiveness and discipline, while the McCain campaign was often disorganised and afflicted by internal disputes.

Oratorical skills and being telegenic

Presidents need to be effective communicators. Great presidents are remembered for great speaking. Here is President Kennedy delivering his Inaugural Address into the frosty air of Washington DC on 20 January 1961:

> Let the word go forth from this time and place, to friend and foe alike, that the torch has been passed to a new generation of Americans — born in this century, tempered

by war, disciplined by a hard and bitter peace, proud of our ancient heritage. Let us begin anew, remembering on both sides that civility is not a sign of weakness, and sincerity is always subject to proof. Let us never negotiate out of fear. But let us never fear to negotiate. And so, my fellow Americans: ask not what your country can do for you — ask what you can do for your country. My fellow citizens of the world: ask not what America will do for you, but what together we can do for the freedom of man.

Such ringing tones have not been heard for over four decades.

Ronald Reagan, too, was a master of oratory, but in a simpler, home-spun way that appealed to ordinary Americans. Here he is talking during the 1980 election about what he saw as an overly powerful and intrusive federal government:

The trouble with this government in Washington is that it works on the following principles: if it moves, tax it; if it keeps moving, regulate it; and if it stops moving, subsidise it. It spends millions of your dollars inventing miracle cures for which there are no known diseases.

It's a clever blend of wit and humour. It may be simplistic, and it's certainly not Kennedyesque, but it can be easily understood by ordinary voters. Contrast this with President Carter, whom Reagan defeated in the 1980 election. When Carter found that his administration had hit the buffers the previous year, he went on television and talked about how he had discovered 'a crisis of the spirit' that was threatening the USA. The speech contained such words as 'fragmentation' and 'immobility' — not in most Americans' lexicons.

The importance of oratorical skills was clearly seen in the 1992 presidential election debates featuring about-to-be-defeated-president George H. W. Bush and about-to-become-president Bill Clinton. Here's an extract from *Newsweek*'s account of just one moment in the second Bush–Clinton debate:

A young black woman asked an awkwardly framed question about how such powerful and sheltered men had been personally affected by the national debt. She meant the recession, not the debt, but only Clinton was quick enough to catch her drift. A puzzled-looking President Bush began his faltering answer with the words which could have served as an epitaph for his entire presidency: 'I don't think I get it,' began Bush. But a few minutes later, Clinton with his touchy-feely gifts at human connection walked up close to the woman, made eye contact with her and spoke meaningfully about being Governor of a poor state in hard times. He knew people who had lost their jobs or their businesses and he felt their pain.

Being telegenic is important. Senator Phil Gramm, running in the 1996 race, stated, honestly, that he was 'too ugly to be president'. Walter Mondale — the losing 1984 Democratic candidate — complained with equal candour: 'I'm no good on television', while his opponent, Ronald Reagan, watching a recording of his own performance, asked immodestly: 'Am I really that good?' Not that being telegenic is always a guarantee of success in presidential elections. Good looks and polished tones did not turn John Kerry into a winner in 2004, and

few people would describe either Richard Nixon or Gerald Ford as 'telegenic'.

Oratorical skills and being telegenic were certainly advantages for Barack Obama in 2008. His campaigning style was compared very favourably with that of his rival in the Democratic primaries, Hillary Clinton, whose speaking style was seen as wooden. Senator Clinton tried to make a virtue of her woodenness, saying that whilst 'we may campaign in poetry, we govern in prose.'

Sound and relevant policies

Some condemn presidential elections as being concerned with style rather than substance — as being policy-free zones — but that is not entirely accurate. Addressing the relevant issues of the day with sound policies can certainly boost a campaign: witness both Bill Clinton and Ross Perot in 1992 on the economy and George W. Bush on moral issues in 2004.

Equally, irrelevant policies are damaging. In 1992, President George H. W. Bush wanted to talk about his foreign-policy achievements, but few voters thought that was the main issue any longer. In exit polls that year, 43% of voters identified 'the economy' as the issue that mattered most in deciding how they voted, while only 8% identified 'foreign policy'. In 2004, John Kerry spent an absurd amount of time talking about the part he played in the Vietnam War, but few voters thought it of any relevance.

The avoidance of sounding whacky or extreme is important too. Barry Goldwater did himself no good at all when, in his acceptance speech at the Republican National Convention in 1964, he declared: 'I would remind you that extremism in the defence of liberty is no vice! And let me remind you also that moderation in the pursuit of justice is no virtue!'

Conclusions

We have identified four constitutional requirements and seven extra-constitutional requirements for becoming president. The winner in most elections is the candidate who scores highest among these extra-constitutional factors. In 2008, McCain bested Obama in political experience (in terms of length of service), but Obama came out top in terms of ability to raise money, organisation, oratorical skills and relevant policies.

Some criticise the selection process for US presidents because they believe it does not test certain presidential qualities, such as an ability to work with Congress. But there is, I would argue, a strong link between many of the qualities that we have identified and those needed in a successful presidency. It is not only in the campaign that one needs effective organisation and oratorical skills. These will help in the White House too. What one needs to *become* president may well assist those who make it. As for the word 'anyone', Barry Goldwater, unsuccessful presidential candidate in the 1964 election, once joked: 'It's a great country: anyone can become president — except me!'

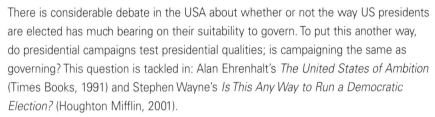

Task 1.1

There is considerable debate in the USA about whether or not the way US presidents are elected has much bearing on their suitability to govern. To put this another way, do presidential campaigns test presidential qualities; is campaigning the same as governing? This question is tackled in: Alan Ehrenhalt's *The United States of Ambition* (Times Books, 1991) and Stephen Wayne's *Is This Any Way to Run a Democratic Election?* (Houghton Mifflin, 2001).

Read the following extracts from these books and then answer the questions which follow.

Source A

I think the system we have today [for selecting presidents] is impossible to justify on a rational basis. I am not trying to insist that it necessarily produces incompetent presidents, or even ones less competent than those some other system might offer us. What can be said about the current process, however, is that it is very likely to produce presidents who lack some of the essential tools for governing. It is now possible to become president without a stable constituency or set of allies even in one's own party. It is very difficult to govern effectively that way. To campaign for president as an individualist, as someone who has risen above factions, interest groups, and entangling alliances, is to court eventual frustration in office.

Alan Ehrenhalt, *The United States of Ambition*, pp. 267–69

Source B

Do contemporary campaigns facilitate or impede governing? Do they provide the skills necessary for elected officials to perform representative and policy-making functions, or do they divert their focus, harden their positions, and convert governing into constant campaigning? They do both.

Similarities

Governing is becoming more campaign orientated. It's increasingly conducted in the public arena; it has become poll driven; a principal motivation for elected officials making public policy decisions is how these decisions will affect their own re-election. Campaign skills are useful for these public aspects of governing. In campaigns, the candidates have to sell themselves and their policies to the electorate. They continue doing so once elected. They have to build support for their

Task 1.1 (continued)

programmes outside government, in order to enhance support for their enactment in government. Presidents must be concerned, like candidates, with their own popularity, because it's thought to contribute to their political influence and subsequent policy successes.

Differences

A campaign is what political scientists call a 'zero-sum game'. If one candidate wins, the other loses. The game's over. The winners no longer have to consider the losers. Government isn't a zero-sum game. For one thing, the losers on a particular issue don't disappear once a battle has been lost. They stay to fight another one. Campaigns need to be run efficiently. Their organisation and operation are geared to one goal: winning the election. In government, although efficiency is desirable, there are other equally important goals. It is often necessary to forge compromise among the contending parties. Candidates are judged by their potential for office. Office holders are judged by their performance in office.

The distinction between running and governing has been exacerbated of late by two recent developments: greater opportunities for those with limited experience to run for office; and the public's mistrust of those in power and its desire for new faces not connected to the current political establishment. Lack of government experience is now regarded as a virtue not a liability. But not only are many non-incumbent candidates neophytes to governing, but their campaign staffs may be as well. The presidential transitions of Carter and Clinton suffered from many staffing inadequacies. The people they appointed to the White House staff came from their campaigns but had little or no experience in Washington politics. Running against the Washington establishment may be an effective campaign strategy. But it's not an effective governing strategy.

Adapted from Stephen Wayne,
Is This Any Way to Run a Democratic Election?, pp. 183–88

(a) Why does Alan Ehrenhalt think that the current system for choosing presidents is 'impossible to justify on a rational basis'?

(b) What evidence does Stephen Wayne suggest for similarities between campaigning and governing?

(c) What is a 'zero-sum game'? Why does Stephen Wayne suggest that, while campaigning is a zero-sum game, governing is not?

(d) Why do you think an 'anti-Washington establishment' strategy is not an effective governing strategy? Can you name any recent presidents who fell victim to this problem?

Task 1.1 (continued)

(e) From the contents of this chapter, Sources A and B, and any other information you have, write a short essay (approximately 300–400 words) in answer to the question:

To what extent do presidential campaigns test the qualities required for the presidency?

Guidance

(a) Look at the last four sentences of Source A.

(b) Look in Source B, in the paragraph entitled 'Similarities'.

(c) Look in Source B, in the first paragraph of the section entitled 'Differences'.

(d) Think about who a president will need to work with once he or she gets to Washington in order to get things done.

(e) • You will need to set out clearly what you think 'presidential qualities' are.

   • To do this, reread the quotation by Cronin and Genovese on page 56 of Anthony J. Bennett's *US Government & Politics* (Philip Allan Updates, 2009, 3rd edition).

   • Remember, presidents will need to bargain with and persuade members of Congress, run a large bureaucracy, make many decisions, rally the country at times of crisis and sell their proposals and policies to ordinary Americans — mostly via televised news conferences or addresses.

   • Remember, too, you are being asked 'to what extent' something is the case. So your answer should not be a straight 'yes, it does' or 'no, it does not' answer.

Further reading

• Ehrenhalt, A. (1991) *The United States of Ambition*, Times Books.
• Wayne, S. (2001) *Is This Any Way to Run a Democratic Election?*, Houghton Mifflin.

Why do presidents bother with the cabinet?

When Barack Obama told his cabinet to 'team up with Taurus of Nemedia' to secure the necessary funding for his programmes in Congress, no one round the table understood what he was talking about. Unlike the President, his cabinet officers are obviously not avid collectors of *Conan the Barbarian* and *Spider-Man* comic books! Maybe the look of incomprehension which the President's remark received was appropriate, as the US president's cabinet itself is a much misunderstood institution. Nowadays it is often seen in studies of the presidency as the poor relation of the much more significant Executive Office of the President (EXOP). But unlike EXOP, the cabinet dates back to the days of George Washington. If it were as useless as some suggest, why would it have survived all this time? What, indeed, did the Founding Fathers have to say about a presidential cabinet?

The founders' intentions

The Founding Fathers decided on a singular executive: 'The executive power shall be vested in *a* President of the United States' [my italics], are the opening 13 words of Article II of the Constitution — the result of a critical decision taken by the members of the Constitutional Convention that began its deliberations in Philadelphia in May 1787. The decision was that the executive power of the USA should be vested in one person, not in a council, or committee, or cabinet. But support for a singular executive was by no means unanimous.

Some of the delegates at Philadelphia had specifically proposed a plural executive. The Virginia Plan, drafted by James Madison, had been ambiguous on this matter, calling for a 'national executive', but the plan put forward by New Jersey lawyer William Peterson called for 'an executive of more than one person', to be elected by Congress. When a singular executive was first openly proposed at the convention, there was, according to Madison, 'a considerable pause of apprehension'. Those against a singular executive, such as Edmund Randolph of Virginia, saw it as 'the foetus of monarchy'. To them, a singular executive conjured up visions of eighteenth-century Britain, of royal governors whose power could not easily be checked, of ermine, crowns and sceptres.

Elbridge Gerry of Massachusetts favoured a single chief executive but also the 'annexing of a Council in order to give weight and inspire confidence'. After all, even the eighteenth-century King of England had a council. But Gerry and oth. saw a plural executive as being unworkable. 'It would be extremely inconvenient in many instances, particularly in military matters,' he stated. 'It would be a general with three heads.' To Alexander Hamilton a plural executive was a recipe for 'feeble' government.

Having written a singular executive into the new Constitution, however, the framers did allow the president to 'require the Opinion in writing of the principal Officers in each of the executive Departments upon any subject relating to the Duties of their respective Offices'. In 1789, there were just three executive departments: State, War (now Defense) and the Treasury. During his first administration, George Washington was unwilling to come to any critical decision without first seeking the advice of these three officers — the secretaries of state, war and the Treasury. The press began to use the term 'cabinet' for the ever more frequent meetings of the president with these three principal officers, usually joined by the Attorney-General.

A question of terminology

When students of UK politics talk about the cabinet, they are undoubtedly talking about the cabinet as a *collectivity* — the cabinet meeting. But this is not necessarily the case in US politics. The term 'cabinet' in US politics refers primarily to the individuals rather than to the meetings. In order to answer the question we have set ourselves — 'why do presidents bother with the cabinet?' — we therefore need to be clear about the terminology.

In posing the question, we are using the word 'cabinet' in the sense of the collectivity — the meeting — because it is in this sense that the usefulness of the US president's cabinet is questioned. We are *not* asking why presidents bother to appoint a secretary of state or secretary of defense, and so on. The answer to that question is obvious. The president bothers with appointing a secretary of state because he needs someone to run the State Department and likewise a secretary of defense to run the Defense Department. The same is true of each of the other 13 heads of executive departments who traditionally make up the collectivity of the cabinet.

The reports we hear about the cabinet *meetings*, where the president and all the 15 heads of executive departments meet around the cabinet table, are usually down-beat. So, the question is why do presidents bother with cabinet meetings?

Conventional wisdom

The conventional wisdom about cabinet meetings is that they are pointless, boring and infrequent events, regarded by many presidents and cabinet officers alike as a necessary evil. Some cabinet meetings undoubtedly fit such a description, but that is probably true of some meetings in any organisation — certainly the ones with which I have been associated. We need to ask whether the US president's cabinet meetings are especially pointless and boring. Specifically, we need to ask whether they are pointless and boring from a president's point of view. Cabinet meetings in the USA have received an almost universally bad press. Do they deserve it?

There is plenty of evidence that some presidents have regarded some cabinet meetings as fairly pointless affairs. President Abraham Lincoln's comment at a cabinet meeting is the most frequently quoted. 'Seven noes, one aye — the ayes have it,' he announced when only he favoured a certain course of action at the end of cabinet discussion. 'I have got you together to hear what I have written down. I do not wish your advice about the matter, for that I have determined for myself,' he remarked when he presented the cabinet with the Emancipation Proclamation to abolish slavery. In more recent times, President Kennedy is on record as describing cabinet meetings as 'boring' and 'a waste of time'.

Not only presidents have been dismissive of cabinet meetings. Here is President Johnson's aide, George Reedy:

> The cabinet is one of those institutions in which the whole is less than the sum of the parts. As individual cabinet officers, the members bear heavy responsibilities in administering the affairs of government. As a collective body, they are about as useful as a worm's appendix. The atmosphere of the cabinet meeting is one which is reminiscent of classroom recitation. There is no such thing as adversary discussion in a cabinet meeting. People do not pound the table, contradict each other, challenge contrary opinions. Whatever fire may have been in their bellies when they entered the White House gate has been carefully quenched by the time they reach the cabinet room door. What follows is a courteous discussion conducted on an extremely high level and enveloped in the maximum dullness conceivable.

The trouble with this conventional wisdom is that Reedy is correct in his conclusion only if he is correct in his belief about what *should* occur in cabinet meetings. Table-thumping cabinet meetings would not necessarily be *useful* cabinet meetings. Have too many criticisms been levelled at cabinet meetings because too much has been expected of them? May it not also be true that derogatory remarks about cabinet meetings are more likely to make the pages of both the newspapers and biographies than if secretary X states that he or she thought the president's cabinet meetings were performing the purpose for which they were intended?

Therefore, we need not only to ask: 'What happens at cabinet meetings?' but also to bear in mind the question: 'What *ought* to happen at cabinet meetings?' We may find that the answer to the question in our chapter title is sometimes the wrong one because people have paid too much attention to the former question and insufficient to the latter.

One further observation before we proceed: the way a president conducts a cabinet meeting — even how often they are held — tells us a good deal about a president's way of doing things. Presidents, like other 'bosses', usually put in place an organisational structure that reflects the way they like to operate. If a president, such as Gerald Ford, feels comfortable with large meetings with wide-ranging topics for discussion, he will adopt a structure to facilitate the holding of such meetings. If, on the contrary, the president prefers meetings with small groups, as did Richard Nixon, then quite a different structure will be used. So, the reasons why a president might still bother to hold cabinet meetings, as well as the frequency with which they are held, reflect the personal preferences and *modus operandi* of each president.

Frequency of cabinet meetings

The conventional wisdom here is that cabinet meetings become less frequent as the presidency continues. While this rule holds for most presidents, it does not hold for all. The reasons for this decline in frequency will become clear as we consider the functions that the meetings can perform, but it is also clear that presidents become busier, especially with the demands of a re-election campaign in their fourth year. Some presidents — notably Jimmy Carter — became so thoroughly disenchanted with their cabinets that meetings later in the presidency must have seemed less attractive. Why hold meetings with people you neither like nor trust?

John Kennedy

During his 34 months in office, Kennedy held 31 cabinet meetings, the first on 26 January 1961, the last on 29 October 1963 — about one per month. This is perhaps more frequently than some commentators have led us to believe.

Stephen Hess, for example, states that Kennedy held cabinet meetings 'as seldom as possible'. That may have been the case, but the impression Hess gives is that Kennedy met his cabinet only three or four times a year. This was not so. The *New York Times* commented a year after Kennedy's election:

> Although it is Washington common-place that President Kennedy doesn't use the cabinet very much, in his [first] nine months in office he has met in formal session with his departmental heads twelve times. In fact, Mr Kennedy's use of the cabinet is sparing only by contrast with that of Mr Eisenhower.

Moreover, it was not necessarily the case that Kennedy was making less *use* of the cabinet just because it was meeting less frequently. It would be quite possible to have a group meeting every day, but not make much use of it. Frequency does not necessarily equal utility.

A noticeable decline, however, took place in the number of meetings held per year, even during this short presidency. Kennedy held 14 meetings in 1961, ten in 1962 and had held only seven by the time of his assassination in late November 1963. According to J. Edward Day, a Kennedy cabinet member, 'the President listened to the group with thinly disguised impatience'.

John Kennedy

Lyndon Johnson

President Johnson, too, held cabinet meetings about once a month. We know, for example, that the 20th meeting of his cabinet took place on 27 July 1965, just 20 months after he became president, but the frequency of Johnson's cabinet meetings increased, rather than declined, during his 5 years in office. There are particular reasons for this. Oddly, Johnson's first full year in office — 1964 — was the year he had to seek re-election. He was also having to meet with a cabinet whose members he had not chosen, and which included his predecessor's brother (Robert Kennedy was still serving as Attorney-General). By 1966, half of Kennedy's cabinet members had gone, replaced by Johnson's own nominees, and, by 1968, only four Kennedy members remained. The number of Johnson cabinet meetings increased year on year: 11, 12, 15, 21 and 22 between 1964 and 1968 — but note that the final year of Johnson's first full term was not consumed in running — he pulled out of the race in late March.

One Johnson cabinet member stated: 'I always went to cabinet meetings thinking, "I wonder how soon I can get away from this so that I can get on with all the work I've got to do." And I think most of my colleagues had the same idea.'

Richard Nixon and Gerald Ford

Little is known of the frequency of Nixon cabinet meetings. Like so much to do with this presidency, there is something of an air of secrecy about it, but we do know that Nixon held 12 cabinet meetings in his first year in office — fewer even than Kennedy. Peter Peterson, who served as commerce secretary from 1972 to early 1973, remembered cabinet meetings being held 'about every 6 weeks'. That would mean only eight or nine per year by that stage of the presidency. He also noted that they became less frequent towards the end of Nixon's first term. Elliot Richardson, a veteran of Nixon cabinet meetings, commented of them: 'Nothing of substance was discussed. There was no disagreement because there was nothing to disagree about. Things over which one might have disagreed were not discussed.'

For the first months of his administration, Gerald Ford held cabinet meetings at roughly 3-weekly intervals. He held 19 cabinet meetings in his first year, something of a record in modern times. There were two particular reasons for this. First, Ford was trying not to be Nixon. Nixon was secretive and operated behind closed doors. Ford wanted to be collegial and open to discussion. Second, Ford had spent a lifetime in the House of Representatives, where he was used to the work of congressional committees; he therefore felt very much at home with the cut and thrust of collegial debate. Cabinet officers remembered cabinet meetings as featuring robust discussion. The secretary to the cabinet, James Connor, for example, spoke about a meeting in which there was a discussion on affirmative action in education: 'All the educators were there — [secretary of state Henry] Kissinger, [secretary of labor John] Dunlop — both were PhDs — and [transportation secretary William] Coleman — a black. It was one hell of a show.'

Jimmy Carter

Jimmy Carter outdid even Gerald Ford in the holding of cabinet meetings. Announcing that he would introduce 'cabinet government' — whatever that meant — Carter scheduled almost weekly cabinet meetings at the start of his administration. In 1977, there were no fewer than 36 cabinet meetings, more than

President Kennedy had held in almost 3 years. But by the beginning of 1978, weekly meetings were being cancelled. 'Well, there goes cabinet government,' joked one cabinet officer. The number of cabinet meetings fell away year on year: 36, 23, 12, 6. National security advisor Zbigniew Brzezinski commented:

> Cabinet meetings were almost useless. The discussions were desultory. There was no coherent theme to them and after a while they were held less and less frequently. They were held on Monday mornings and so as not to completely waste my time, I would spend the time catching up on my reading of the weeklies [such as *Time* and *Newsweek*] carefully hidden on my knees below the edge of the cabinet table.

Ronald Reagan

Much the same thing happened in the Reagan White House. Reagan, too, chalked up 36 cabinet meetings in his first year, but the remainder of his first term saw a falling off, with 21 in 1982 and 12 each in 1983 and 1984. But defense secretary Caspar Weinberger, who served through all but the last year of Reagan's 8 years, remembered that 'certainly the number of full cabinet meetings diminished during the 7 years I served'. Transportation secretary James Burnley stated that by 1988 — Reagan's last year in office — the holding of cabinet meetings had 'all but dried up' and that the secretary to the cabinet 'struggled to think up an excuse to have one'.

Education secretary Terrel Bell remembered Reagan cabinet meetings for reasons other than to do with policy:

> As the President sat down at the start of the cabinet meeting, he reached over to the centre of the table to pull a jar of jelly beans his way. He selected jelly beans from the jar and then passed it on to [defense secretary] Casper [*sic*.] Weinberger. As the jar came round, each cabinet member selected a few beans.

George H. W. Bush

The first Bush White House learnt from those who had served under Reagan not to overdo the cabinet meeting. 'Use them sparingly,' warned secretary of state James Baker, who had served as White House chief of staff and then secretary of the Treasury in the Reagan administration, 'and don't turn them into a dog and pony show.' One Bush cabinet member remembered: 'Very often they were a waste of time; you could get very bored.'

Bill Clinton

The low point of cabinet meeting use came during the presidency of Bill Clinton. Clinton much preferred to work through informal groups and disliked the formality of the cabinet meeting. There were only six cabinet meetings in

Clinton's first year, and in 1998 — his sixth year in office — there were just two, both centring on the Monica Lewinsky affair.

Labor secretary Robert Reich wrote in his memoir, mischievously entitled *Locked in the Cabinet* (1997):

> The first cabinet meeting in months. We sit stiffly while Bill talks about current events as if he were speaking to a group of visiting diplomats. I've been in many meetings with him, but few with the entire cabinet, and it suddenly strikes me that there's absolutely no reason for him — for any president — to meet with the entire cabinet. Cabinet Officers have absolutely nothing in common, except the first word in their titles. Maybe Bill is going through the motions because he thinks that presidents are supposed to meet with their cabinets and the public would be disturbed to learn the truth.

George W. Bush

Like his father before him, George W. Bush had been warned against overdoing cabinet meetings. 'This president has experience — as a state governor, as well as from his father — to know the pitfalls to avoid,' stated the secretary to the cabinet, Albert Hawkins, just 4 weeks into Bush's first term. Bush held 49 cabinet meetings in 8 years, but there was none of the huge fluctuations in the number of meetings per year seen in the Reagan and Carter years. There were never more than nine in a year (2001) and never fewer than four (2007). Bush held cabinet meetings at particular moments to coincide with 'big-ticket' events: the State of the Union Address; the submission of the budget to Congress; upcoming midterm elections, to give three examples.

Not all reviews of the meetings were kind. Former Treasury secretary Paul O'Neill, in his curiously entitled memoir *The Price of Loyalty*, described a Bush cabinet meeting as being 'like a blind man in a room full of deaf people'.

Barack Obama

At the time of writing (the summer of 2009) it's rather early days to make any definitive remarks about the frequency and regularity of President Obama's cabinet meetings. Obama was initially prevented from holding cabinet meetings because of the length of time it took him to assemble the entire team after problems in filling the posts of secretary of commerce and secretary of health and human services. Thus his first meeting was held on 20 April 2009, a full 3 months to the day since Obama had taken office. Obama's predecessor held his first cabinet just 11 days into his presidency and had held two more meetings by early April. A White House press release on the morning of 20 April 2009 stated:

President Obama will hold the first cabinet meeting of his Administration this morning. As part of his commitment to go line by line through the budget to cut spending and reform government, he will challenge his cabinet to cut a collective 100 million dollars in the next 90 days. Agencies will be required to report back with their savings at the end of 90 days.

The Obama cabinet convened again on 8 June, 7 weeks later. However, one unusual occurrence between these two meetings was the holding of weekly 'cabinet meetings' chaired by Vice-President Joe Biden. The Vice-President alluded to these meetings in a press briefing in the White House State Dining Room before the 8 June meeting:

> Mr President, a couple of weeks ago, you authorised me, and I thank the Cabinet for doing this, to call a Cabinet meeting once a week. A couple of weeks ago, I asked the Cabinet members to give me a list of new projects that they were absolutely certain of they could get up and running in the second hundred days that would build momentum and accelerate the job growth in the next hundred days.

These early meetings concentrated exclusively on the economy, jobs, the passage of the Economic Recovery Act and the so-called 'Roadmap to Recovery'. In this sense, Obama was following his predecessor's pattern of holding cabinet meetings to discuss big-ticket items which affected all cabinet members, rather than discussing policy minutiae. But different presidents hold cabinet meetings for different reasons.

Reasons for a president to hold cabinet meetings

These much-maligned meetings do, in fact, serve a number of important functions for the president. There are, therefore, several reasons why presidents bother with the cabinet.

They can engender team spirit

Unlike a new administration in the UK, the members of a new US cabinet might not know each other or the president very well. There is no shadow cabinet in the US system of government. In addition, with a strict separation of personnel between the legislature and the executive, membership of the legislature will not provide a common bond for cabinet members as it does in the UK. So, especially at the beginning of a presidency, cabinet meetings are important for engendering team spirit. They are 'get-to-know-you' sessions.

They allow presidents to appear collegial and consultative

This was particularly important in the post-Watergate era. Nixon was notorious for not liking cabinet discussion. So those presidents who came after him wanted to appear collegial and consultative. In his autobiography, *A Time to Heal*, Gerald Ford, Nixon's immediate successor, wrote:

> On Saturday, my second day as president, I convened the cabinet. Nixon had always behaved rather formally with his cabinet, seldom shaking hands or exchanging banter. He got down to business very quickly. It's pretty hard to change your style at 61 and I had no intention of changing mine. I strode into the room and shook hands all round.

Even such gestures are important. In this sense, a cabinet meeting is something of a public relations exercise. Robert Reich raised the same point when he wrote that President Clinton 'thought that presidents are supposed to meet with their cabinets'. President George W. Bush always invited the press in at the end of a cabinet meeting. The photo opportunity was an important method whereby the president acknowledged that he was meeting with the cabinet.

They provide opportunities for both giving and gathering information

Presidents are busy people and so are their cabinet officers. Getting the 15 heads of the executive departments — the giants of the federal bureaucracy — in a room and telling them things is an efficient way of disseminating information. It is more efficient than sending round memos or e-mails. The minutes of a meeting record precisely what was said and to whom. If someone later claims not to know something, the president can merely state: 'You were at the meeting.' It saves the president having the same conversation with 15 different people on 15 separate occasions.

It is also a good way for the president to find out what's going on around the vast federal bureaucracy. President Carter insisted on cabinet members submitting, before each meeting, a written report on what they had achieved in their department since the last meeting. He would then go round the table asking questions. President Obama has used cabinet meetings for getting cabinet officers to both propose budget cuts and job creation schemes to cope with the economic downturn faced by the nation at the start of his presidency.

They provide a forum for policy debate

This is among the most important of cabinet functions. True, most cabinet officers are policy specialists and there is no doctrine of collective responsibility, but many policy debates do not fit neatly into one department's portfolio; they are more commonly cross-departmental issues. Here's an example from the first President Bush's administration, as remembered by cabinet secretary David Bates:

At the cabinet meeting prior to the Malta Summit [with Soviet President Mikhail Gorbachev in December 1989], the President engaged the cabinet in a very significant discussion of foreign policy. I think the cabinet values the opportunity to present their views directly and candidly. The pre-Malta cabinet meeting allowed the President to broaden his consultations. Cabinet Officers such as [Veterans' Affairs Secretary] Ed Derwinski or [HUD Secretary] Jack Kemp may naturally not have been included in the detailed briefings that preceded the Malta trip, but they have travelled overseas frequently, have broad policy experience and have clear and useful views that augment what the President had learned elsewhere.

They provide opportunities for 'team talks' and presenting 'big picture' items

This is how President George W. Bush saw cabinet meetings. Bush scheduled cabinet meetings just before — or sometimes just after — a significant political event. He then used the cabinet meeting to give a kind of 'pre-match' talk to his 'team' and present 'big picture' items like the federal budget. The second cabinet meeting of his first term was held on 26 February 2001 — the day before he made his first speech to a joint session of Congress. The next was held on 9 April — the day he presented his first budget to Congress. The same year, there was a meeting on 14 September — 3 days after the terrorist attacks on New York and Washington. He held a cabinet meeting on 2 August 2004 — the day the 9/11 Commission published its recommendations. The President went straight from the cabinet meeting to the Rose Garden to make his first public response to the report. Two days after the 2004 elections, he called a cabinet meeting to review the agenda for his second term. We have already seen that this is how President Obama uses his cabinet.

They allow a president to check up on legislation going through Congress

Here is another obvious and important function of cabinet meetings. Unlike the UK prime minister, the US president does not bump into cabinet members in the legislature. Neither the president nor those in the cabinet are members. Yet the cabinet members are critical players in the president's liaison with Congress on key items of legislation. The president will want them to lobby Congress for the passage of those bills that are a priority. What better way of checking up on how things are proceeding than in a cabinet meeting? George W. Bush used cabinet meetings to push for congressional action on such legislation as the Homeland Security Bill (24 September 2002), Medicare reform (9 June 2003) and the federal budget (5 April 2005). Here is George W. Bush speaking with members of the press straight after the 13 July 2005 cabinet meeting:

I told Congress and I told the country we'd cut the deficit in half by 2009. We're ahead of projections now. And so my message to the United States Congress is, let's be wise with taxpayers' money. Over the next couple of weeks I look forward to working with Congress to continue pro-growth policies. One is getting an energy bill. Secondly, is to promote free and fair trade. And finally, we want to work with Congress to pass a fiscally responsible highway bill.

They allow presidents to see cabinet members they wouldn't otherwise see

We have already alluded to this. Neither the president nor those in the cabinet are members of Congress. They therefore have no other way of meeting than at meetings that the president sets up. Whereas the president might have a number of one-on-one meetings with 'first-tier' cabinet members, such as the secretary of state or the secretary of defense, 'second-tier' cabinet members, such as the secretaries of education or transportation, rarely get to see the president. Jack Knebel, who served as secretary of agriculture in the Ford cabinet, tells how he was contacted by his successor in the Carter administration, Bob Bergland, who complained that he 'didn't get to have so much as a cup of coffee with the President'. This is how Clayton Yeutter, the first President Bush's agriculture secretary, put it:

[Cabinet meetings] were useful for being informative. You got an insight on the top stories. It was for some just the thrill to have a meeting with the President. The 'second tier' cabinet officers don't get to see him that often. They would go back to their departments and be able to say: 'I just came from a cabinet meeting.' They would then hold their own staff meetings and the message [from the cabinet meeting] would be passed out to sub-cabinet people and so to the rest of the department. They were evangelistic.

Conclusions

Cabinet meetings are potentially of great use to the president and to the cabinet members. They can fulfil key functions that will enable the president to be more successful both in relations with Congress and in managing the vast federal bureaucracy. Some presidents — notably Reagan and the first George Bush — have used sub-cabinet groups known as cabinet councils as well. These operate as more policy-focused groups.

Writing a few years after leaving the White House, former president Gerald Ford had this to say about the cabinet:

I am a strong believer in an effective Cabinet. That means that you cannot rely on political flunkies. But if a president has good cabinet heads, he can delegate a lot of authority. He does not have to get into the minutiae of running the federal government.

Former president Richard Nixon took a quite different view. Writing 6 years after his resignation, Nixon said:

> Every new president takes office promising a strong Cabinet of independent members, and some new presidents take office really believing this promise. But each soon learns that the Cabinet as a collective body is not suited to decision making.

Presidential scholar Nelson Polsby recently commented that the trouble with being a member of the president's cabinet is that, 'although you get a seat at the table, the table doesn't get used'. I'm not sure I entirely agree. The table might not get used for making decisions, but that's not its purpose. We have identified seven important cabinet functions that *are* conducted around it, and for those reasons, presidents are right to bother with it.

Task 2.1

Read the following extracts and then answer the questions that follow.

Source A

Lloyd Bentsen's first year as Clinton's treasury secretary wasn't exactly the epitome of Cabinet clout. His advice to President Clinton to compromise on an economic stimulus package was rejected. He disagreed with Hillary Rodham Clinton on health care reform, and lost that battle too. His plan to consolidate banking regulation, with less than total White House backing, faltered. His influence in domestic policy-making gradually diminished.

Bentsen was — still is — a victim of an important un-remarked feature of the Clinton presidency: the chief executive has largely ended the Cabinet as we know it. Though former presidents had already downgraded the Cabinet as an institution, Clinton has virtually abolished it. The full Cabinet doesn't meet often. When it does, not much happens.

The meetings, designed to be substantive, hardly advanced the administration's agenda. Example: on a sunny day last October, the 14 department heads with Cabinet rank and the 7 others with Cabinet 'status' wandered across Pennsylvania Avenue from the White House to Blair House. They were joined by Clinton and Vice-President Al Gore for lunch and two hours of unstructured discussion. Before the gathering, Christine Varney, the Cabinet coordinator at the White House, had privately encouraged everyone to tell President Clinton whatever was on his mind. Few did. The discussion dwelt on the North American Free Trade Agreement (NAFTA). The meeting was all talk and no deliberation. Nothing was decided. There was no agenda to act on. No policy or political strategies were set.

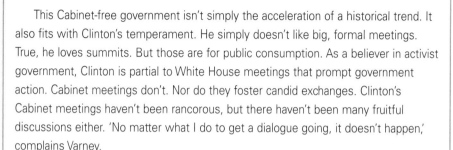

Task 2.1 (continued)

This Cabinet-free government isn't simply the acceleration of a historical trend. It also fits with Clinton's temperament. He simply doesn't like big, formal meetings. True, he loves summits. But those are for public consumption. As a believer in activist government, Clinton is partial to White House meetings that prompt government action. Cabinet meetings don't. Nor do they foster candid exchanges. Clinton's Cabinet meetings haven't been rancorous, but there haven't been many fruitful discussions either. 'No matter what I do to get a dialogue going, it doesn't happen,' complains Varney.

Clinton prefers to deal with Cabinet members in small groups or individually. Cabinet sessions are 'idling time', says Housing Secretary [Henry] Cisneros. Like Clinton, he thinks the Cabinet, operating as a body, is obsolete. Still, meetings are scheduled. Cabinet members must set aside the last Friday and Monday of each month in case the President wants to gather them. Normally, he doesn't.

Adapted from Fred Barnes, 'Cabinet losers',
New Republic, 28 February 1994

Source B

Several Clinton White House leaders observed that they would like to have seen some rejuvenation of the old-style cabinet meetings — with the boss. Commented one:

I found people need to be touched and seen and heard — by the President. He is an incredible communicator. I think it would be good for him to talk to his own people. He does it ad hoc; he sees them all the time at events, but I would suggest to him that they have a meeting, at the very least, once a quarter — something fairly regular. They can get inspired by it. What happens, you see, is they turn around and when they go to Detroit the next day they can say, 'I was just with the President.' It's a little awkward when they are not getting to say that. It is nice when they can tell people, 'The President asked me yesterday to make sure you understand this is important for our economy, for our country.' I would do a little more of that.

Adapted from Bradley H. Patterson, *The White House Staff:
Inside the West Wing and Beyond* (**www.americanpresident.org**)

(a) What evidence is there in Source A that President Clinton did not value the meeting of the full cabinet?

(b) What factors, according to Fred Barnes, are said to have influenced Clinton in reaching the conclusion that 'the Cabinet, operating as a body, is obsolete'?

(c) Why does the anonymous Clinton cabinet member quoted in Source B think it would be good to have some old-style cabinet meetings?

Chapter 2

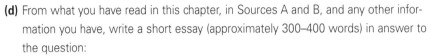

Task 2.1 (continued)

(d) From what you have read in this chapter, in Sources A and B, and any other information you have, write a short essay (approximately 300–400 words) in answer to the question:

Examine the advantages and disadvantages of holding cabinet meetings.

Guidance

(a) You will need to focus on the second paragraph in Fred Barnes's article.

(b) The quotation itself is taken from the last paragraph. But the answer comes in the third and fourth paragraphs.

(c) There are really two reasons: one for the benefit of the cabinet members themselves and another for the benefit of the president in terms of what cabinet members might do *after* a cabinet meeting.

(d) • Remember you have been asked to 'examine', not just list or describe. To 'examine' is to subject something to careful scrutiny, study and criticism.

• Before you write your answer, draw up a table with two columns — one headed 'advantages', the other headed 'disadvantages'. This will form the basis of your essay plan.

• When coming to a final conclusion, remember that it is not necessarily the *number* of advantages or disadvantages that you need to consider, but how *important* they are. Arguments need to be *weighed*, not just *counted*.

Further reading

• Bennett, A. J. (1996) *The American President's Cabinet*, Macmillan.
• Patterson, B. H. (2000) *The White House Staff: Inside the West Wing and Beyond*, Brookings.
• Reich, R. (1997) *Locked in the Cabinet*, Knopf.

How can presidents win in Congress?

The Capitol

To ask the question 'How can presidents win in Congress?' is to realise just how fundamentally different the relationship between the US president and Congress is from the relationship between the UK prime minister and Parliament. I suppose the answer to 'How can UK prime ministers win in Parliament?' is simply: by getting a good overall majority and maintaining party discipline. Ask Tony Blair, who during the first 8 years of his premiership did not suffer a single defeat on the floor of the House of Commons. A US president would be hugely envious of such control over the legislature.

This is mostly due to the difference between the separation of powers (or, more accurately, the separation of institutions) in the USA and the fusion of powers in the UK. In the UK, the prime minister is part of the legislature. More than that, he or she is the leader of the majority party in the House of Commons in what is a *de facto* unicameral system. In the USA, the president cannot be a serving member of the Congress. When Barack Obama won the presidency in 2008, he had to resign from the Senate. If there is a vote of no confidence in

the House of Commons, the whole government can be swept away, as Jim Callaghan's Labour government was in 1979, but in the USA, there is no way Congress can get rid of 'the government'. True, it can remove individual members of the executive branch, through impeachment (in the House) and trial (in the Senate), but, even if the president were impeached, tried and removed from office, the vice-president would merely step up to take over. Had Bill Clinton been removed following impeachment in the late 1990s, Al Gore would have become president. It's all so very different.

The US president cannot *command* Congress. Presidents must lead, bargain and compromise. Presidential power is the power to persuade. Presidents' *powers* may help, but their *power* — their ability to get Congress to do what it wouldn't otherwise do — is decided largely by their ability to persuade. Ronald Reagan was famously labelled as 'the Great Communicator', but according to David Broder, the eminent *Washington Post* columnist, a better description of Reagan was 'the Great Persuader'. What we shall be finding out in this chapter is: what makes a great persuader? Before we do that, let's just remind ourselves of those powers that should facilitate presidential success, for, as Richard Neustadt reminds us, although 'powers are no guarantee of power', 'powers may lead to power'.

Presidential powers

The president has seven powers that are relevant to his relationship with the Congress. Four of these concern legislation.

First, the president can propose legislation to Congress. Most obviously, he does this in the annual State of the Union Address. Presidents use this speech to try to set the agenda of Congress for the coming year. As political scientist Charles Jones wrote:

> Since it is not possible to treat all issues at once, members of Congress and others anxiously await the designation of proprieties. These presidential choices are typically from a list that is familiar to other policy actors. Nonetheless, a designator is important, even if he is a Republican having to work with a Democratic Congress. As in any organisation, there is a need for someone in authority to say, 'Let's start here.'

Second, the president can submit an annual budget to Congress. This will be done with some fanfare — a news conference maybe, a ceremony in the Rose Garden or the East Room at the White House, a meeting with the full cabinet.

Third, the president can sign bills into law, and, fourth, he can veto legislation. The threat of the veto can also be used as a bargaining tool during the legislative process. Because Congress knows that the president nearly always wins with a veto — it is very difficult, and rare, for Congress to override the president's veto (see Table 3.1) — Congress will often make changes in legislation to satisfy the president, if it can thereby avoid the president using the power of veto.

Table 3.1 **Presidential vetoes, 1933–2009**

President	Party	Dates	Regular vetoes	Pocket vetoes	Total	Number of vetoes overridden	Percentage of vetoes overridden
Roosevelt	D	1933–45	372	263	635	9	1.4
Truman	D	1945–53	180	70	250	12	4.8
Eisenhower	R	1953–61	73	108	181	2	1.1
Kennedy	D	1961–63	12	9	21	0	0.0
Johnson	D	1963–69	16	14	30	0	0.0
Nixon	R	1969–74	26	17	43	7	16.3
Ford	R	1974–77	48	18	66	12	18.2
Carter	D	1977–81	13	18	31	2	6.5
Reagan	R	1981–89	39	39	78	9	11.5
Bush (41)*	R	1989–93	29	15	44	1	2.3
Clinton	D	1993–2001	37	1	38	2	5.3
Bush (43)**	R	2001–09	0	0	0	0	0.0

*George H. W. Bush, 41st President
**George W. Bush, 43rd President

Presidents have three further powers that impinge upon their relationship with Congress. They may nominate executive branch officials. They may nominate federal judges. They may negotiate treaties with foreign powers. All three powers require confirmation or ratification by the Senate.

Thus we can see that presidential powers make the president heavily dependent upon Congress when he needs to get things done. So, what conditions might facilitate presidential success in Congress? And what are the methods of persuasion presidents can use, to help them get their way with Congress?

Circumstances

There are a number of circumstances that, if they exist, will probably help a president to get his way in Congress. We shall consider these circumstances in more detail in the final chapter, when we answer the related question, 'What makes a good president?' So I will only list them here.

First, it should help a president to get his way with Congress if he is popular. Popularity can be measured in two different ways: the size of the president's victory in the last election and the monthly approval ratings, which are researched and published by leading polling and media organisations such as Gallup and ABC News. Big election victories and high approval ratings should help a president win in Congress. Even after his relatively narrow victory in 2004, President George W. Bush talked of 'spending his political capital'.

Second, having both chambers of Congress controlled by the president's own party should assist presidential success. In this respect, George W. Bush had more favourable circumstances than did his father. Divided government — the White House and Congress under the control of different parties — became very much the norm for the period between 1969 and 2009, as shown in Table 3.2. During that 40-year period, divided government was the order of the day for all but just over 10 years. Conversely, in the previous 40-year period between 1929 and 1969, united government was in evidence for all but 10 years.

Table 3.2 Partisan control of the presidency and Congress since 1933

Dates	Presidents	Party	Party controlling Congress
1933–47	**Roosevelt/Truman**	**D**	**D**
1947–49	Truman	D	R
1949–53	**Truman**	**D**	**D**
1953–55	**Eisenhower**	**R**	**R**
1955–61	Eisenhower	R	D
1961–69	**Kennedy/Johnson**	**D**	**D**
1969–77	Nixon/Ford	R	D
1977–81	**Carter**	**D**	**D**
1981–87	Reagan	R	Split
1987–93	Reagan/Bush (41)	R	D
1993–95	**Clinton**	**D**	**D**
1995–2001	Clinton	D	R
2001 (Jan–May)	**Bush (43)**	**R**	**R**
June 2001–03	Bush (43)	R	Split
2003–06	**Bush (43)**	**R**	**R**
2007-09	Bush (43)	R	D
2008–	Obama	D	D

Third, a crisis can rally Congress — and the country — round the president, leading to presidential success. We can see this clearly in George W. Bush's first term in its pre- and post-9/11 manifestations. The attacks on New York and Washington in September 2001 enhanced the circumstances in which the president would probably get his way with Congress. Having said that, crises whose cause might be laid at the president's door, or unavoidable crises that are then mismanaged, might have the opposite effect. Nixon's Watergate affair (1973–74) and Carter's Iranian hostage crisis (1979–81) are examples of these two situations. Clearly, Nixon and Carter were hugely hindered, rather than helped, by these respective crises.

Persuasion

Essentially, presidents get their way with Congress through persuasion. Presidents can use other people to work for them in Congress as well as employing various forms of persuasion themselves.

The people used by the president

There are four categories of people the president can use in trying to succeed with Congress.

First, there is the vice-president. The vice-president is the only member of the executive branch who has a foothold in the legislature because of his role as president of the Senate. In this role, the vice-president can chair Senate debates and vote in the case of a tie. The vice-president rarely, if ever, performs the first, and the second comes round only occasionally, but when it does it is of critical importance in winning the day for the president. In April 2001, just 3 months into the Bush presidency, Vice-President Dick Cheney used this power twice in a 48-hour period, first to pass legislation on prescription drug benefit and then to increase a proposed tax cut in an effort to eliminate the 'marriage penalty'. In May 2003, Cheney again broke a tied vote to pass a $350 billion tax cut, the centrepiece of the president's legislative agenda that year. In 2005, during a debate on a ban — which the White House opposed — on 'cruel, inhuman or degrading' treatment of detainees in US custody, Cheney personally telephoned all 55 Republican senators to seek their support. On this occasion, however, the vice-president's words fell on mostly deaf ears. The amendment authorising such a ban was passed by the Senate by 90 votes to 9. In 2009, just hours before the Senate vote on Obama's $787 billion stimulus bill, it was Vice-President Joe Biden who tracked down the elusive Pennsylvania senator Arlen Specter. Biden

called White House chief of staff Rahm Emanuel with the news: Specter would vote 'yes'.

It helps that so many recent vice-presidents have had previous experience in Congress. Table 3.3 shows that, of the 12 vice-presidents who have held office since 1953, ten have previously served in Congress. In the 1980s Dick Cheney rose to be the Republican whip in the House of Representatives — the second-highest-ranking minority post in the House. Nixon, Johnson, Humphrey, Ford, Mondale and Biden all served lengthy and distinguished periods of service in Congress before graduating to the vice-presidency. Therefore, vice-presidents will often find themselves talking with former colleagues and dealing with a legislative process that they understand thoroughly. Joe Biden and Arlen Specter had served together in the Senate for 28 years before that conversation about the stimulus bill in April 2009. That counts for a lot.

Table 3.3 Previous congressional service of vice-presidents since 1953

Vice-president	Dates	Previous congressional service?
Richard Nixon	1953–61	Yes
Lyndon Johnson	1961–63	Yes
Hubert Humphrey	1965–69	Yes
Spiro Agnew	1969–73	No
Gerald Ford	1973–74	Yes
Nelson Rockefeller	1974–77	No
Walter Mondale	1977–81	Yes
George H. W. Bush	1981–89	Yes
Dan Quayle	1989–93	Yes
Al Gore	1993–2001	Yes
Dick Cheney	2001–09	Yes
Joe Biden	2009–	Yes

In a *Washington Post* article ('Taking the Hill', 7 June 2009), Matt Bai reported:

Part of Biden's White House portfolio is to act as unofficial ambassador to the Senate, carrying information back and forth between his old colleagues and his new boss. During the recent debate over the budget, he walked onto the Senate floor and sat himself down, uninvited, next to Senator Max Baucus, the Montana Democrat, who as chairman of the powerful Senate Finance Committee will be a central figure in the coming healthcare debates. Biden [also] described working out at the Senate gym as vice-president and stopping by the Senate dining room alone for a bowl of soup. He was amazed, he said, when his former colleagues lined up to say hello.

Such informal contacts are invaluable for a president seeking success in Congress.

Second, the president will look to the staff of the Office of Legislative Affairs, which is part of the White House staff within the Executive Office of the President. Their ability to work the corridors, committee rooms and offices of Capitol Hill will be decisive in whether or not the president wins or loses on crucial votes. The person given the job of leading this office must be efficient, persuasive, well informed and knowledgeable about the way things work in Congress. Some have served their presidents very well indeed, such as Nicholas Calio for George W. Bush during his first term. Some have proved more of a hindrance than a help. During the Carter presidency, the following joke circulated in Washington: 'What's the difference between the President's congressional liaison staff and the Boy Scouts?' The answer: 'The Boy Scouts operate under adult supervision.' It is important that such contacts are seen as a two-way street: to misquote JFK, it is a case of 'ask not [only] what members of Congress can do for you, but what you can do for them'.

Third, the president will look to the cabinet and key White House staffers. Many of the legislative proposals that the president backs are specifically linked with a particular executive department. When President George W. Bush was pushing his huge 2003 tax cut, Commerce Secretary Don Evans and Treasury Secretary John Snow were both used by the President to lobby House and Senate members, as were economic adviser Stephen Friedman, and Office of Management and Budget Director Mitch Daniels. Don Evans and John Snow, for example, made a round of calls on members of the Senate Finance Committee to push the president's tax cut proposals.

In the Obama administration, White House chief of staff Rahm Emanuel — himself a former member of the Democratic leadership team in the House of Representatives — is a key player in liaison with Congress. In the same *Washington Post* article cited above, Matt Bai commented:

> Obama's aggressive courtship of Congress is plotted and directed by Emanuel, who despite his legendary personality flaws — his penchant for profane mockery is now so well documented that you sometimes have the sense that he's cursing at you so as not to disappoint — is freakishly well suited to the job. Emanuel served as a senior aide in Clinton's White House before running for Congress and then overseeing the Democrats' successful drive [in 2006] to take back the House, which means he is that rare politician who feels equally at home on both ends of Pennsylvania Avenue. 'Rahm is family to us all,' Nancy Pelosi, the House Speaker, told me recently.

Fourth, the president will look to the party leadership in Congress to work among their colleagues. On the same tax cut, the Republican leader in the

Senate, Bill Frist, was at the White House twice in 3 days, accompanied by other key Senate Republicans, and House speaker Dennis Hastert was mobilised to urge support for the President.

The methods used by the president

In trying to persuade members of Congress to support presidential proposals, the president can use a number of methods. It's not as crude as a favour for a vote. Much of this 'activity' is merely creating an atmosphere in which persuasion is more likely to be successful. If the president ignores you for months, or even years, and then suddenly asks you to cast a difficult vote in favour of a certain proposal, the request is likely to fall on deaf ears. If, however, you were recently wined and dined at the White House, at least your predisposition is more likely to be favourable.

A president might phone members of Congress. I remember once being in the office of Congressman Charles Bennett (no relation) of Florida when a call came through from President Reagan. Congressman Bennett immediately stood up! The President was calling to ask for his support on an upcoming vote. I accompanied the congressman to the members' dining room for lunch later in the day, and he was happy to announce to anyone in earshot that he'd taken a call from the President. It was indeed something of an honour. But presidents must use such methods sparingly. To do otherwise is to cheapen them.

A president might invite members of Congress to the White House — either for a business meeting or for a purely social engagement, either in a group or individually. A working breakfast at the White House, a meeting in the cabinet room, a one-on-one with the president in the Oval Office are all possibilities. Ronald Reagan often invited members of Congress to call by to watch a movie with him. In the George W. Bush White House, the invitation was more likely to be to a barbecue. On 4 April 2001, President Bush met with members of the Congressional Hispanic Caucus for a 45-minute meeting in the cabinet room to discuss potential policies on immigration, education and the economy. At a formal White House dinner given in honour of the Prince of Wales and the Duchess of Cornwall in early November 2005, the guest list included not only House speaker Dennis Hastert and Senate majority leader Bill Frist, but also two Democrats, Senator Joe Lieberman of Connecticut and Congresswoman Jane Harman of California. Small courtesies are important. On 15 December 2005, the President met in the Oval Office with Republican senators John McCain of Arizona and John Warner of Virginia to discuss the administration's position on the interrogation of suspected terrorist detainees. At the start of his administration, Barack Obama began holding Wednesday-night cocktail parties at the White House for members of Congress.

As Chief of Staff in the Obama administration, Rahm Emanuel believes in putting to good use what he calls 'the strategic assets' of the White House. As the *Washington Post* reported:

> There's the White House theater, where guests can watch movies and sporting events; formal state dinners; smaller gatherings in the first family's residence, which spouses can join; tickets to the Easter-egg roll for kids; tickets to the White House tours that members of Congress can give out to the constituents. These prizes are not handed out randomly or, as in the Bush White House, doled out mostly as rewards to allies who've demonstrated the requisite loyalty. Rather, in the Obama administration, they are considered carefully and accounted for obsessively. Emanuel holds a daily legislative meeting at which aides discuss the status of pending legislation, and often they go over the distribution of White House assets during those sessions. 'We have a tracking system,' Emanuel states. 'Who came to watch the football game? Who came to watch the basketball game?'

Within the first 4 months of the Obama administration, some 320 House members and about 80 senators had visited the White House, a quite extraordinarily level of courtship of Congress by the President. And although some invitations were to White House events with the President, others were for one-on-one meetings in the Oval Office. Senator Max Baucus of Montana, who had such an Oval Office meeting with Obama, was clearly impressed, saying that it implied equality between the executive and legislative branches of government and enabled Obama to establish personal relationships more quickly. 'You been hunting lately?' Obama asked Senator Ben Nelson of Nebraska as he walked into the Oval Office and found himself, much to his surprise, alone with the President.

Something that a president might be able to offer to fellow party members of Congress is to campaign for them in the next round of congressional elections. This is especially useful for House members who represent districts not usually on the itinerary of a serving president. The following story was told to me by the late Republican congressman Steve Schiff of New Mexico:

> President Bush's staff told me that he would be in Albuquerque at 10 o'clock in the morning on a certain day during the 1992 election campaign. 'You'll be there?' the President's men had asked. I agreed that I would be. But later, I was contacted by the Bush folk. The President's itinerary had changed and he'd now be stopping off in Salt Lake City and so would not now arrive in Albuquerque until 4 in the afternoon. But I had to explain that I was due back in Washington to vote and the last plane left Albuquerque at 4 o'clock. Word came back that I should miss the plane. 'But what about my getting back to Washington?' I asked. 'We'll see to that,' said the Bush staff. I remained in Albuquerque, appeared with the President and then flew back to Washington aboard Air Force One with the President.

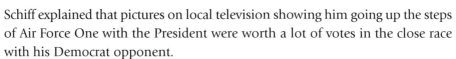
Schiff explained that pictures on local television showing him going up the steps of Air Force One with the President were worth a lot of votes in the close race with his Democrat opponent.

While I was spending time in the early 1990s with the Republican senator Mark Hatfield of Oregon, the senator's chief of staff Steve Nousen told me that Hatfield enjoyed a close relationship with President George H. W. Bush. According to Nousen, Bush would ask, 'What do you need?' What he got was federal money to help complete a new light rail/tram system for Portland, the state's premier city. In return for his support of Obama's 2009 economic stimulus bill, Arlen Specter, who has Hodgkin's disease, won a large increase in cancer research funding for the National Institutes of Health.

Joseph Pika in *The Politics of the Presidency* (2006) puts it like this:

> Bestowing or denying favours to members of Congress gives presidents a measure of leverage. Such favours may be given to an individual member or to important people in his or her constituency, or the favor may be of benefit to the constituency itself. Favors given as rewards to members of Congress include appointments with the president and other high-ranking officials; letters or telephone calls from the president expressing thanks for support; campaign assistance in the form of cash from the party's national committee, a presidential visit to the constituency, or a presidential endorsement; the opportunity to announce the award of federal grants to recipients in the constituency; invitations to be present at bill-signing ceremonies, to attend White House social functions, and to accompany the president on trips; and White House memorabilia such as pens and photographs. To some extent, all members of Congress share in such benefits, but the president's supporters have readier access to them and feel more comfortable asking for them than do others.

If all else fails, presidents might use their final weapon — to appeal over the heads of members of Congress by going on nationwide television. This is a risky strategy, which an unpopular president would adopt at his or her peril. Rather than galvanise support, it can merely help to guarantee failure, thus further diminishing the president's power to get things done. A lower-risk strategy would be to use the weekly radio address — something that has become a regular Saturday fixture since Ronald Reagan reintroduced it to great effect in the 1980s. Such television and radio appearances allow the president to appeal directly to ordinary Americans, no longer dependent — as they are in television news or newspapers — on the 'filter' of the reporter, presenter, editor or other journalist. Here's President George W. Bush in his weekly broadcast on 17 December 2005, appealing for support in his bid to get Congress to renew the 2001 Patriot Act:

> The key provisions of this law are set to expire in 2 weeks. The terrorist threat to our country will not expire in 2 weeks. The terrorists want to attack America again, and inflict even greater damage than they did on September 11th [2001]. Congress has a

responsibility to ensure that law enforcement and intelligence officials have the tools they need to protect American people. The House of Representatives passed reauthorisation of the Patriot Act. Yet a minority of senators filibustered to block the renewal of the Patriot Act when it came up for a vote yesterday. That decision is irresponsible and it endangers the lives of our citizens. The senators who are filibustering must stop their delaying tactics and the Senate must vote to reauthorise the Patriot Act.

The results of persuasion

The results of presidential persuasion should be that presidential legislation is passed — largely in the form in which the president wanted it. Furthermore, the president's budgets will be passed, nominations confirmed, treaties ratified and vetoes sustained. The extent to which these things occur is measured in the annual presidential support score.

There is a strong of correlation between high presidential support scores and united party control of government. Table 3.4 shows that of the years with the ten highest support scores, eight were years of united party control of the presidency and Congress. In the other 2 years, the president had control of at least one chamber for that year. It is noticeable that 5 of these 10 years represent the first full year of a particular presidency. This suggests that the so-called 'honeymoon period' still has some effect.

Table 3.4 **Ten highest presidential support scores, 1953–2008**

Presidential support score (%)	Year	President	Party	Party controlling Congress
93.1	1965	Johnson	D	D
89.2	1953*	Eisenhower	R	R
87.9	1964*	Johnson	D	D
87.8	2002	Bush (43)	R	R
87.1	1963	Kennedy	D	D
87.0	2001*	Bush (43)	R	Split
86.4	1993*	Clinton	D	D
86.4	1994	Clinton	D	D
85.4	1962	Kennedy	D	D
82.4	1981*	Reagan	R	Split

*First year in office.

On the other hand, Table 3.5 shows that all the years showing the ten lowest support scores were years of divided government. Note that 4 of these 10 years

coincide with a particular president's last year in office. A further 4 years — 1999, 2007, 1987 and 1959 — coincide with the president's penultimate year in office. Now the honeymoon has given way to the lame duck.

Table 3.5	Ten lowest presidential support scores, 1953–2008			
Presidential support score (%)	Year	President	Party	Party controlling Congress
37.8	1999	Clinton	D	R
38.3	2007	Bush (43)	R	D
43.0	1992*	Bush (41)	R	D
43.5	1987	Reagan	R	D
46.8	1990	Bush (41)	R	D
47.4	1988*	Reagan	R	D
47.8	2008*	Bush (43)	R	D
50.6	1973	Nixon	R	D
52.0	1959	Eisenhower	R	D
53.8	1976*	Ford	R	D

*Last year in office.

There is some evidence to suggest that this link between presidential success in Congress and united government continues in terms of the confirmation of the president's appointments and the ratification of the president's treaties in the Senate. Table 3.6 shows that recent high-profile defeats of presidential appointments and treaties have all come at times of divided government.

Table 3.6	Partisan control of the presidency and Senate coinciding with recent high-profile rejections of appointments/treaties by the Senate			
Year	Rejection	President	Party	Party controlling Senate
1969	Haynesworth to Supreme Court	Nixon	R	D
1970	Carswell to Supreme Court	Nixon	R	D
1987	Bork to Supreme Court	Reagan	R	D
1989	Tower as Defense Secretary	Bush (41)	R	D
1998	White to district (trial) court	Clinton	D	R
1999	Nuclear Test Ban Treaty	Clinton	D	R

Conclusions

How, then, can presidents win in Congress? Given that all presidents come to office with the same set of formal powers, essentially the same tools of persuasion and much the same resources in terms of White House personnel, what accounts for their varied levels of success? We have certainly found that partisan control of Congress can be critical. So, too, are presidential popularity and the stage that presidents have reached in their term of office — better a honeymoon than a lame duck.

But there are other variables, too. Gerald Ford and Jimmy Carter both came to the Oval Office at a time of congressional re-assertiveness. The presidency was a relatively weak office following the debacles of Watergate and Vietnam. This was not a difficulty that arose for either Lyndon Johnson or George W. Bush. Personality is another important variable. Reagan, Clinton and Obama had the advantages of being gregarious extroverts to whom people often warmed. Nixon and Carter had no such advantages.

Legislative skill is another factor. Johnson and Nixon had honed their skills at dealing with Congress through many years of experience serving in both chambers. Carter and Clinton had no such experience upon which to draw, and it often showed.

As Nelson Polsby in *Congress and the Presidency* (1976) has wisely reminded us:

> Conflict and co-operation between Congress and the president are not merely the result of whim or wilfulness at one end or the other of Pennsylvania Avenue. There are institutional reasons that make it difficult for Congress and the president to see eye to eye.

James Madison, as one of the nation's Founding Fathers, made it clear in *The Federalist* No. 51 that the constitutional framers wanted presidential–congressional conflict:

> To what expedient shall we finally resort for maintaining in practice the necessary partition of power among the several departments, as laid down by the Constitution? The only answer that can be given is by so contriving the internal structure of the government as its several constituent parts may, by their mutual relations, be the means of keeping each other in their proper places.

Thus, the Founding Fathers built conflict into the system through its checks and balances — its 'separate institutions, sharing powers', as Richard Neustadt so neatly expresses it. We must remember that, when we see conflict between the White House and Capitol Hill, the correct response is not so much 'Who's to blame?' as 'How can we work round it?' A president who uses a combination of formal powers, informal persuasion, popularity and legislative skill, and is fortunate enough to be in favourable circumstances — having a clear mandate and united government — can hope to get many proposals through Congress.

Cronin and Genovese (2004) state: 'Leadership is difficult [in the USA] precisely because the framers of the Constitution wanted it to be so.' They remind us that 'opportunities to check power abound; opportunities to exercise power are limited'. It's difficult for the president to win in Congress. It's meant to be. In trying to get their way, they must constantly bear in mind what James Pfiffner in *The Modern Presidency* (St Martin's Press, 2000) reminds us: that 'presidents cannot command obedience to their wishes, but must persuade'.

Task 3.1

Study Table 3.1 on page 41 and write a paragraph about presidential vetoes.

Guidance

- You could, for example, work out an average number of presidential vetoes during a 4-year presidential term by adding the figures in column 6 (Total) and dividing this figure by the number of years, then multiplying by four.
- It might be interesting to do this for different periods, such as: for each president; for Republican and Democrat presidents separately; and for the period 1933–2009. You could do your calculations for regular vetoes and pocket vetoes separately.
- You could work out the average percentage of regular vetoes overridden during the period 1933–2001. Add up the figures in column 4; add up the figures in column 7; divide the second figure by the first figure; multiply by 100.

Task 3.2

Read Source A, an article which appeared in the *Washington Post* in 1998, and answer the questions that follow.

Source A

President Clinton and Vice-President Gore publicly appealed to House Republicans yesterday to consider any 'compromise' to head off the fateful impeachment vote slated for later this week.

Three House Republicans who had been on a White House target list of undecided members announced yesterday that they will vote to impeach Clinton when the issue reaches the floor [of the House of Representatives] on Thursday and several others were poised to follow suit as early as today. Another key moderate who was one of only a handful of Republicans to oppose impeachment, Rep. Christopher Shays of Connecticut, signaled he was reconsidering and asked to meet with Clinton. Vice-President Gore canceled an out-of-town trip and prepared to

Task 3.2 (continued)

contact House Democrats. To limit defections, Gore plans to call important House Democrats.

As the debate reached fever pitch, switchboards at the Capitol were swamped by thousands of calls while congressional e-mail systems crashed under the load of constituent messages.

Well-funded interest groups geared up as well. The AFL-CIO has begun a full-bore drive to stop impeachment, calling on members to contact their representatives and to join anti-impeachment demonstrations. The AFL-CIO has set up a toll-free number that members can call to be transferred to their House member's office. People for the American Way, another liberal advocacy group, will begin airing radio advertisements today to solicit callers.

Meanwhile, Clinton — the subject of all the frenetic activity — remained half a world away. During an unprecedented presidential visit to Gaza yesterday, Clinton was again confronted with questions about impeachment and called on congressional leaders to allow a vote on a censure resolution that would reprimand him but leave him in power.

With the President out of the country at the most inopportune moment, White House advisers were at a loss to devise a winning strategy. A few think Clinton should make another speech, perhaps even travel to Capitol Hill to address the House in person. Others urge him to invite groups of moderates to talk with him privately. Some even hold out hope for help from first lady Hillary Rodham Clinton.

Republicans currently control the House, 228 to 206, with one independent who caucuses with the Democrats. Three Democrats have indicated that they will or are likely to vote to impeach Clinton, while five Republicans have gone in the other direction.

Adapted from Peter Baker and Juliet Eilperin,
'Clinton and Gore appeal to Republicans for compromise',
Washington Post, 15 December 1998

(a) List all the groups which were in any way lobbying members of Congress on the President's behalf.

(b) List all the methods mentioned in the article which President Clinton either had used or might use to lobby members of Congress, either collectively or individually.

(c) What role was Vice-President Gore playing in this operation?

(d) Describe the nature and volume of contacts being made by constituents to their House members.

(e) What role were interest groups playing?

(f) The article tells us that President Clinton was in the Middle East at this time. Why do you think he might have decided to go ahead with this trip?

Task 3.2 (continued)

(g) From the data presented in the last paragraph, how many more Republican House members did the President need to persuade to support him in the vote in order to avoid being impeached?

Guidance

(a) There are two different groups of people — look in paragraphs 3 and 4.

(b) There are certainly four different methods mentioned in the article.

(c) Look in paragraphs 1 and 2 of the article.

(d) This is in paragraph 3.

(e) This is all in paragraph 4. The AFL-CIO is the American Federation of Labor-Congress of Industrial Organizations, a kind of US equivalent of the Trades Union Congress (TUC) in the UK.

(f) It might help you to know that presidents in a personal crisis often like to go abroad. For example, as the Watergate scandal was breaking, President Nixon went off on a well-publicised trip to the People's Republic of China. How do you think such presidents want to appear by taking such trips? What message are they trying to convey back home?

(g) This is just a bit of simple maths. Democrats: 206 + 1 – 3 + 5; Republicans 228 – 5 + 3. I'll leave the rest to you!

Further reading

- Cronin, T. E. and Genovese, M. A. (2004) *The Paradoxes of the American Presidency*, Oxford University Press.
- Pfiffner, J. (2005) *The Modern Presidency*, Thomson Wadsworth.
- Pika, J. (2006) *The Politics of the Presidency*, CQ Press.
- Polsby, N. (1976) *Congress and the Presidency*, Prentice-Hall.
- Woodward, B. (2004) *Plan of Attack*, Simon and Schuster.

What happened to the imperial presidency?

The origin of the term 'the imperial presidency'

The term 'the imperial presidency' gained popularity in the early 1970s as a consequence of Arthur Schlesinger's book of that title. Schlesinger, a former aide to President Kennedy and a distinguished historian, published *The Imperial Presidency* in 1973. In this book Schlesinger charts what he saw as the abuse of power by successive twentieth-century presidents, but most especially by Lyndon Johnson (1963–69) and Richard Nixon (1969–74). This abuse of power was made all the more dangerous, claimed Schlesinger, because the US presidency had grown so much since the 1930s.

When Franklin Roosevelt became president in March 1933, the executive branch of the federal government was staffed very modestly indeed. But once the Executive Office of the President (EXOP) was formed in 1939, the president's personal bureaucracy grew hugely. Indeed, its growth paralleled the growth of the executive branch as a whole — itself a consequence of both the New Deal and the USA's expanded role in foreign policy both during and after the Second World War. The White House would now incorporate powerful new offices such as the National Security Council and the White House staff. What's more, Congress had very little control over this personal bureaucracy. Most posts within EXOP were not subject to Senate confirmation.

Critics of this presidential enlargement saw the White House as coming to resemble a royal court, with the president as a latter-day emperor. With the power of the federal executive enhanced and the size of the federal executive enlarged, presidents became less accountable, more secretive and at times downright illegal. These characteristics of the modern presidency — unaccountable power, secrecy and illegality — were to Schlesinger the hallmarks of the imperial presidency. Presidents Johnson and Nixon personified the imperial presidency in the crises of Vietnam abroad and Watergate at home. 'The imperial presidency' referred to a version of US government in which the conventional checks and balances between the three branches of government — and especially those between the executive and the legislature — had got out of balance. The executive branch had become dominant; the legislature had become subservient.

According to Schlesinger, 'the imperial presidency was essentially the creation of foreign policy'. At times of crisis abroad, the US people in general, and even Congress itself, look to the president for leadership. The USA was in a continual state of war — hot or cold — from the early 1940s to the early 1990s. This allowed successive presidents to take advantage of the ambiguities and uncertainties of the Constitution in terms of the war-making powers.

The founders' intentions

Because the theory of the imperial presidency hinges so much on the president's role in using troops abroad, we need to understand the debate surrounding the writing of the Constitution on this matter. In the Constitution, as the Founding Fathers designed it, the president lacks the authority to initiate military action. The president is 'commander-in-chief of the army and navy', but Congress is given the power to declare war. According to Gene Healy:

> In the Framers' view, [in the absence of] a congressional declaration of war, the president's war powers would be purely reactive: if the territory of the United States or US forces were attacked, the president could respond. Barring that, he could not operate without congressional authorisation.
>
> 'Arrogance of power reborn: the imperial presidency and foreign policy in the Clinton years', *Policy Analysis*, 13 December 2000

In August 1787, in the midst of the Philadelphia Convention, the Founding Fathers considered a recommendation that Congress should be given the sole power 'to make war'. Only one delegate of the 55 present spoke in favour of giving this power to the president. George Mason of Virginia stated that he was against giving the president war-making powers because he 'could not be trusted with it'. But the problem with giving Congress the war-making power was that Congress was seen as too large and met too infrequently to supervise the details of conducting a war. It was for this reason that James Madison proposed to insert the word 'declare' instead of the word 'make', 'leaving to the president the power to repel sudden attacks'. Another delegate, Roger Sherman, thought this proposal 'stood very well' — that the president should 'be able to repel and not to commence war'. The motion was passed with Madison's amendment.

So the Constitution that emerged from the Philadelphia Convention contained an important, but very limited, role for the president in war-making. The president's only power, stated in Article II, was that:

> The President shall be Commander-in-Chief of the Army and Navy of the United States, and of the Militia of the several States, when called into the actual Service of the United States.

It gave almost all the war-making powers to Congress:

> To declare War; grant Letters of Marque and Reprisal, and make Rules concerning Captures on Land and Water; to raise and support Armies; to provide for calling forth the Militia to execute the Laws of the Union, suppress Insurrections and repel invasions.

To summarise, the Constitution granted the power to *initiate* military action to Congress, while granting the power to *supervise* military action to the president. Congress's role was to be *proactive*; the president's role was to be *reactive*. This was all done for a purpose. You will recall that the Founding Fathers were fearful of executive power — of tyranny. James Wilson, another of the Founding Fathers, thought the strength of the arrangement they had created regarding war powers was that:

> This system will not hurry us into war. It is calculated to guard against it. It will not be in the power of a single man, or a single body of men, to involve us in such distress. For the important power in declaring war is vested in the legislature at large.

Even Alexander Hamilton, himself a great supporter of a strong executive, reassured his fellow New Yorkers that the president, however strong he might be, would not have the monarchical power to lead the nation unilaterally into a war. Although the president's authority as commander-in-chief would be 'nominally the same as the King of Great Britain, [it would be] in substance much inferior to it'. Hamilton continued:

> It would amount to nothing more than the supreme command and the direction of the military and naval forces, while that of the British King extends to the declaring of war.

Even readers with a casual knowledge of the US presidency over the past half-century will appreciate how much presidents such as Harry Truman (Korea), Lyndon Johnson (Vietnam) and Richard Nixon (Cambodia) have extended their war-making powers from those intended by the Founding Fathers. It is this extension — some would say abuse — of presidential war-making powers that is at the very heart of the debate about the imperial presidency.

The birth of the imperial presidency

In periods of peace and tranquillity, Americans look to Congress for leadership. At such times the people in general, and Congress in particular, feel confident to challenge and check the president. But in times of threat and instability, Americans look to the president for leadership. Both they and Congress feel that the 'president has the facts'. The executive branch can use various devices, such as executive privilege and the secrecy surrounding government agencies like the CIA, to keep the citizenry and Congress in the dark.

During the first century and a half of the republic, there was little opportunity for executive dominance. Wars against Great Britain (1812), Mexico (1846–48), Spain (1898) and Germany (1917–18) were the only foreign engagements. Add to those the American Civil War (1861–65) and one sees that during the first 150 years of the nation's history, from 1789 to 1939, the USA was engaged in war for only 11 years.

In contrast, the last 60 years in US history have seen a continual state of international conflict and crisis. These times of crisis have enabled successive presidents to increase incrementally their war-making power. The Japanese attack on Pearl Harbor in December 1941 allowed Franklin Roosevelt to break free from congressional restraint, once Congress had exercised its constitutional right to declare war — the last time it did so. As David Mervin (*Ronald Reagan and the American Presidency*, 1990) commented:

> The age of crisis was well underway and the constitutional balance of powers [between the president and Congress] would never be the same again.

When, in 1950, North Korea invaded South Korea, President Truman immediately sent US troops to support South Korea and, on the advice of his secretary of state, Dean Acheson, did not seek congressional authorisation for this war-making. The State Department argument was that:

> The president, as Commander-in-Chief of the Armed Forces of the United States, has full power of the president to use the armed forces of the United States without consulting Congress.

Commenting on this incident, Arthur Schlesinger stated in *The Imperial Presidency*:

> Korea beguiled the American government first into an unprecedented claim for inherent presidential power to go to war and then into ill-advised resentment against those who dared bring up the constitutional issue. 'The circumstances of the present crisis,' an executive document sourly said in 1951, 'make any debate over prerogatives and power essentially sterile, if not dangerous to the success of our foreign policy.' By

insisting that the presidential prerogative alone sufficed to meet the requirements of the Constitution, Truman dramatically enlarged the power of future presidents to take the nation into major war.

In 1958, President Eisenhower sent 14,000 US troops to Lebanon, without any congressional authorisation. The abortive Bay of Pigs invasion of Cuba by US-backed Cuban exiles was planned by the Eisenhower administration and carried out under the Kennedy White House in 1961; again, there was no congressional approval. Congress played no role in the Cuban Missile Crisis the following year, either. Kennedy had been not only Schlesinger's boss — Schlesinger served as a White House adviser — but also his hero. Later, Schlesinger bemoaned the way the Kennedy administration had handled the Cuba crisis. It had set a bad precedent. 'What should have been celebrated as an exception was instead enshrined as a rule,' he later wrote. According to Schlesinger, the imperial presidency reached its apogee during the presidencies of Johnson and Nixon.

Johnson's 'rampant' presidency

In 1964, during the Vietnam War, Congress passed an authorisation — the Tonkin Gulf Resolution — which stated:

> Congress approves and supports the determination of the President, as Commander in Chief, to take all necessary measures to repel any armed attack against the forces of the United States and to prevent further aggression.

The House voted for the resolution unanimously and in the Senate only two dissenting voices could be heard. This wasn't so much a power grab by President Johnson as an abdication of power by Congress. It was a blank cheque that Johnson took as the moral and legal equivalent of a declaration of war. By the time Lyndon Johnson left the White House in January 1969, the USA had over half a million troops in Vietnam. This, in Schlesinger's words, was 'the rampant presidency'. Congress had been reduced to a mere spectator.

Lyndon Johnson

Schlesinger quotes a congressional veteran, Carl Vinson of Georgia, who had been elected to the House of Representatives in 1914. It was Vinson's view that the role of Congress

> has come to be that of a sometimes querulous but essentially kindly uncle who complains while furiously puffing on his pipe but who finally, as everyone expects, gives in and hands over the allowance, grants the permission, or raises the hand in blessing, and then returns to his rocking chair for another year of somnolence broken only by an occasional anxious glance down the avenue and a muttered doubt as to whether he had done the right thing.

Some might see this as an apt description of Congress over George W. Bush's Iraq adventure 35 years later.

Nixon's 'revolutionary' presidency

Under Richard Nixon, the imperial presidency was characterised not only by war-making in Vietnam and Cambodia, but also by the Watergate affair, 'enemies lists', illegal use of the CIA, bugging, wire-tapping and claims of executive privilege. Nixon's overly centralised and overly secretive White House turned political opponents into enemies and attempted to interfere with both the democratic and the judicial processes. This, in Schlesinger's words, was 'the revolutionary presidency'.

But it was also the period when Congress fought back to reclaim some its rightful powers. It passed some significant pieces of legislation in an attempt to curb presidential power. The Case Act (1972) required the president to submit all executive agreements to Congress in an attempt to prevent presidents making secret agreements with foreign powers. The War Powers Act (1973) attempted to clarify the roles of both Congress and the president in war-making. The Congressional Budget and Impoundment Control Act (1974) attempted to strengthen Congress's role in the budget-making process. In the same year, the House Judiciary Committee drew up Articles of Impeachment against President Nixon, precipitating his resignation.

Thus, a US president was brought down by his own hubris and by Congress. That the epitome of the imperial presidency had been brought down with comparative ease — even before the House of Representatives had debated the Articles of Impeachment, much less had passed them and sent the case for trial by the Senate — raises a number of interesting questions about the imperial presidency thesis. Was the imperial presidency all that it was made out to be by Schlesinger and his supporters? Surely, if it could be ended with such ease and rapidity, we might need to question the existence not only of the emperor's new clothes, but of the emperor himself?

The imperilled presidency

Within 6 years of Nixon's departure, his immediate successor, Gerald Ford, would be suggesting that the presidency, far from being 'imperial', was now 'imperilled'. By 1980, the USA might be said to have had four successive 'failed' presidencies — Lyndon Johnson, Richard Nixon, Gerald Ford and Jimmy Carter. None had managed to complete a second term in office. The last two hadn't even been elected to a second term.

Writing in *Time* magazine on 10 November 1980, the week after Jimmy Carter's defeat, Gerald Ford mused about the office of the presidency:

> Some people used to complain about what they called an 'imperial presidency', but now the pendulum has swung too far in the opposite direction. We have not an imperial presidency but an imperilled presidency. Under today's rules, which include some misguided 'reforms', the presidency does not operate effectively. That is a very serious development, and it is harmful to our overall national interests.

Gerald Ford had served for 24 years in the House of Representatives before serving just over 3 years in the White House — first as vice-president and then as president — so he had a good perspective from which to look at the relationship between the legislative and executive branches of the federal government.

> The biggest change since I first went to Washington has been the revision in the relationship between the presidency and Congress. Immediately after World War II the presidency was at its peak; the Congress was very responsive, especially in foreign policy. Today a president really does not have the kind of clout with the Congress that he had in the 1950s, even in matters of national security.

Ford identified two reasons for this changed relationship: the erosion of party leadership in Congress and the inability of successive presidents to control the federal bureaucracy. Ford's recommendations were: to beef up the powers of the party leadership in Congress; to make greater use of both the vice-president and the cabinet; and for presidents to spend more time with members of Congress.

These comments by ex-president Ford serve to remind us that presidential power is not a constant, but is cyclical. The history of the presidency over the 25 years since Ford made these comments has been one of further peaks and troughs in presidential power.

Reagan and the post-imperial presidency

It is an irony that Gerald Ford coined the phrase 'the imperilled presidency' in an article that appeared on the eve of Ronald Reagan's election to the presidency. Reagan (1981–89) would become the first president since Eisenhower (1953–61) to complete two terms in office. His dominance of Washington politics quickly led to another revision of the theory of presidential power. Reagan achieved this dominance despite the fact that his own Republican Party never controlled the House of Representatives throughout this 8-year period, and controlled the Senate only for the first 6 years of his presidency.

The major event over which Reagan's use of presidential power was questioned was what became known as the Iran–Contra affair. This foreign policy fiasco centred on the role of Colonel Oliver North in the White House's two-pronged plan of selling arms to Iran and channelling funds to the Contra rebels in Nicaragua, both policies being in contravention of congressional bans. It also brought into question the roles of White House chief of staff Donald Regan and national security advisor John Poindexter, both of whom lost their jobs as a result.

Congress set up a joint select committee to look into the whole affair, and the committee report was revealing in its conclusions. It was the committee's view that the ingredients that had led to this debacle bore an eerie resemblance to those that had become associated with the imperial presidency. According to the majority report:

> The common ingredients of the Iran and Contra policies were secrecy, deception and disdain for the law...

> The Constitution gives important powers to both the president and the Congress in the making of foreign policy. Yet in the Iran–Contra affair administration officials holding no elected office repeatedly evidenced disrespect for Congress's efforts to perform its constitutional oversight role in foreign policy...

> [National security advisor John] Poindexter testified to his efforts to keep the covert action in support of the Contras from Congress: 'I simply did not want any outside interference. [National Security Council staff member Colonel Oliver] North testified: 'I didn't want to tell Congress anything' about this covert action...

> Several witnesses stated or implied that foreign policy should be left solely to the president, arguing that shared powers have no place in a dangerous world. But the theory of our Constitution is the opposite. Circumvention of Congress is self-defeating for no foreign policy can succeed without the bipartisan support of Congress.

George H. W. Bush and the cooperative presidency

George H. W. Bush had witnessed the Iran–Contra affair during his time as vice-president in the Reagan White House. He clearly was not going to repeat the errors during his own presidency. The post of national security advisor (NSA) was returned to that of policy coordinator rather than policy initiator. His NSA was Brent Scowcroft, who had been a member of the Tower Commission (which had written its own independent report on the Iran–Contra business). Bush was determined to handle Congress differently, seeing it as an equal partner in foreign policy making.

So when, in 1990, Bush faced his stiffest foreign policy test with the Iraqi invasion of Kuwait, he adopted the style of the presidency recommended in the congressional select committee report. Bush wanted bipartisan support on Capitol Hill before sending troops into Kuwait to repel the Iraqi invasion. He asked Congress to pass a resolution approving of military action in Kuwait — a resolution that passed the House of Representatives by 250 votes to 182 and the Senate by 52 to 47. President Bush's Republicans were joined by 86 Democrats in the House and 10 Democrats in the Senate.

Congressional authorisation having been given, the conduct of the 44-day campaign showed that, once hostilities begin, it is the president who, in Alexander Hamilton's phrase, has 'the supreme command and the direction of the military forces'. During the campaign itself, Congress was variously described as 'feeling extremely helpless' and 'left on the sidelines'. President Bush would summon the congressional leadership team to the White House for regular briefings, but there was no doubt at all that decision making was entirely in the hands of the President and his small team of advisers — chairman of the joint chiefs of staff Colin Powell, national security advisor Brent Scowcroft, secretary of state James Baker and secretary of defense Dick Cheney.

Clinton: an imperial presidency?

One of the problems with the term 'imperial presidency' is that it lacks a clear definition. It has too easily become a label that is stuck on virtually any modern presidency by its critics. Some people seriously argued that even the administration of Bill Clinton fitted the soubriquet of 'imperial presidency'. In the 13 December 2000 edition of *Policy Analysis*, Gene Healy, a noted Washington attorney, published an article entitled, 'Arrogance of power reborn: the imperial presidency and foreign policy in the Clinton years'. I have used many adjectives to describe the Clinton presidency, but never 'imperial'. In the article, Healy concentrated on two areas in which he regarded Clinton as an imperial president: the treaty-making power and the war-making power. Let us briefly consider each in turn.

Article II, section 2, of the Constitution states that the president 'shall have power, by and with the advice and consent of the Senate, to make treaties, provided that two-thirds of the Senators present concur'. Clearly, this wording is not beyond debate. How does one define the Senate's power to give 'advice and consent'? As is often the case with such

Bill Clinton

constitutional debates, the Founding Fathers help us. In *The Federalist* No. 69, Alexander Hamilton refuted the argument that the Constitution had given the president the same treaty-making powers as the British monarch. Whereas the British monarch was 'the sole and absolute representative of the nation in all foreign transactions', the US president would merely share in the treaty power with the Senate. Thus, argued Hamilton:

> There is no comparison between the intended power of the president and the actual power of the British sovereign. *The one can perform alone what the other can only do with the concurrence of a branch of the legislature* [my italics].

Healy argued that, when it came to the Comprehensive Test Ban Treaty (CTBT), President Clinton adopted a patently unconstitutional position. Clinton had signed the CTBT in 1996 which, if ratified by the Senate, would have bound the USA to refrain indefinitely from underground testing of nuclear weapons (above-ground testing had already been banned since 1963). But, when the President sent the treaty to the Senate, the Senate stalled for 2 years and eventually rejected it by a 48–51 vote, 18 votes short of the two-thirds majority required for ratification. Five days after this Senate defeat, however, the Clinton administration asserted that the treaty was still in force. In a letter dated 18 October 1999, secretary of state Madeleine Albright wrote to the foreign ministers of other signatory nations that 'despite this setback, I want to assure you that the United States will continue to act in accordance with its obligations as a signatory under international law'. It would have been quite proper for Secretary Albright to assure her fellow foreign ministers that the USA, despite the Senate refusal to ratify, was not about to conduct underground nuclear testing, but it was the phrase about 'obligations as a signatory under international law' that raised some eyebrows. Healy stated:

> Secretary Albright was mistaken. The United States has no obligations as a signatory to the treaty. Under the Constitution, the United States has no *obligation* to abide by a treaty that the Senate has rejected.

Healy went on to argue that the Clinton administration had taken a similar position on the Kyoto Protocol.

We have already considered the Founding Fathers' intent regarding war-making powers. In the absence of a congressional declaration of war, it was their intention that the president's role be merely reactive — if the territory or forces of the USA were attacked. But President Clinton pursued military action — undeclared wars — in Haiti, Bosnia and Serbia, as well as making surprise air strikes on Sudan, Afghanistan and Iraq. In Serbia, for example, the US-led NATO forces flew more than 37,000 sorties between March and June 1999. When presidential spokesman Joe Lockhart was asked whether this constituted a war, he replied:

> No. And we believe that the United States' objectives here are not offensive or aggressive in aim, and constitute the limited use of force to meet clear objectives. We certainly do not consider ourselves to be at war with Serbia or its people.

The following exchange took place in another press conference:

Q: Is the President ready to call this a low-grade war?

Lockhart: No. Next question.

Q: Why not?

Lockhart: Because we view it as a conflict.

Q: How can you say that it's not a war?

Lockhart: Because it doesn't meet the definition as we define it.

The White House might have made the same response to questions about whether or not the President 'had sexual relations with that woman, Ms Lewinksy' — 'No, because it doesn't meet the definition as we define it.' According to Gene Healy, 'the Clinton administration espoused a view of executive war-making authority that [was] as unconditional and unconstrained as that claimed by any president in American history'. In Healy's view, Clinton's administration therefore qualified to be labelled an 'imperial presidency'.

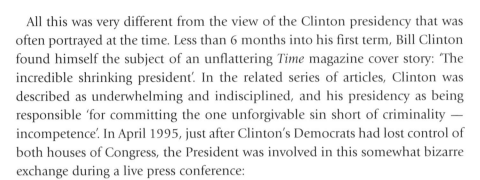

All this was very different from the view of the Clinton presidency that was often portrayed at the time. Less than 6 months into his first term, Bill Clinton found himself the subject of an unflattering *Time* magazine cover story: 'The incredible shrinking president'. In the related series of articles, Clinton was described as underwhelming and indisciplined, and his presidency as being responsible 'for committing the one unforgivable sin short of criminality — incompetence'. In April 1995, just after Clinton's Democrats had lost control of both houses of Congress, the President was involved in this somewhat bizarre exchange during a live press conference:

> Q: Mr President, hasn't the forcefulness with which [the Republican] majority in Congress is pursuing its agenda pushed your priorities to the side-lines or made them irrelevant?

> *President:* No. The Constitution gives me relevance; the power of our ideas gives me relevance; the record we have built up over the last 2 years and the things we're doing to implement it give it relevance.

A newspaper cartoon the next day showed a US living room scene. An over-size television that seemed to fill the entire room was showing President Clinton shouting, 'But I am relevant!' In front of the television were two things: a large sofa, completely empty, and a cat on the rug — asleep. It didn't look much like the imperial presidency. In addition, Arthur Schlesinger — the originator of the phrase — didn't seem to think much of the idea of Clinton as an imperial presidency. An article he wrote in the *New York Times* on 3 August 1998 was entitled 'So much for the imperial presidency'.

George W. Bush and the imperial presidency reborn?

It was undoubtedly the Bush administration's military operations in Iraq that led some of George W. Bush's critics to reach for the 'imperial' adjective. 'Bush acting as imperial president' was the headline of a Helen Thomas article syndicated in Hearst newspapers on 3 July 2002, which the sharp-penned Ms Thomas opened with the line: 'The imperial presidency has arrived.' The *Christian Science Monitor* carried an article by Dante Chinni on 11 March 2003 entitled 'The imperial presidency is back — but who's watching?' On 28 June 2003, Arthur Schlesinger had another article — this time in the *Washington Post* — entitled 'The imperial presidency reborn'. Schlesinger claimed that the 'Bush doctrine' of preventive war was clearly unconstitutional. He wrote:

> The Bush doctrine transfers excessive power to the president. Abraham Lincoln long ago foresaw the constitutional implications of the preventive war policy. On February 15, 1848, he denounced the proposition 'that if it shall become necessary to repel invasion, the president may, without violation of the Constitution, cross the line and invade the territory of another country'. Lincoln continued: 'Allow the president to invade a neighbouring nation, whenever he shall deem it necessary to repel an invasion, and you allow him to make war at pleasure. The Founding Fathers resolved to so frame the Constitution that no one man should hold the power of bringing this oppression upon us.' If the Bush doctrine prevails, the imperial presidency will surely be reborn.

Maureen Dowd in a *New York Times* article later the same year claimed that Bush and his supporters wanted to 'bring back the imperial, imperious presidency'.

However, things quickly changed. In October 2005, an article in *The Economist* entitled 'Et tu, Brute?' had this to say:

> This autumn's most gripping television series, HBO's *Rome*, tells the story of how Julius Caesar tightened his grip on power in the capital of the world's greatest empire. In the new Rome — Washington DC — on the banks of the Potomac, exactly the opposite is happening: George Bush's iron grip on power is loosening as more and more Washingtonians join the revolt against the imperial presidency.

Some commentators believe that the force behind the move towards increased presidential power in the Bush administration was Vice-President Dick Cheney rather than the President himself. Cheney's political career was born in the immediate aftermath of the Watergate affair and the resignation of President Nixon. As a young White House chief of staff to President Ford, Cheney saw the presidency at one of its weakest moments — an unelected president (who had not even been elected as vice-president) hemmed in by a resurgent Congress. For the next 25 years, Cheney continued to believe that the presidency was a weakened — imperilled — institution, and he saw his coming to the vice-presidency as an opportunity to restore presidential power to what, in his view, was its proper constitutional standing in the federal system of checks and balances.

According to Andrew Rudalevige, author of *The New Imperial Presidency* (2005), the presidency had recovered its status and power long before Cheney returned to the White House in January 2001. Those pieces of presidency-curbing legislation passed in the 1970s, which Cheney regarded as a mistake — such as the Case Act, the War Powers Act and the independent counsel statute — had either been discarded or manoeuvred around by the time of the Bush presidency.

Bruce Fein, a constitutional lawyer and Reagan administration official, claimed in a *Washington Post* article that Cheney is 'living in a time warp'. According to Fein, 'The great irony is that Bush inherited the strongest

presidency of anyone since Franklin Roosevelt, and Cheney acts as if he's still under the constraints of 1973 and 1974.' Even Republican senator John Sununu of New Hampshire, whose father acted as White House chief of staff to George W. Bush's father, said that 'the Vice-President may be the only person I know of that believes the executive has somehow lost power over the last 30 years'.

President George W. Bush claimed that his assertions of presidential authority were only a response to the events of 11 September 2001. At a mid-December 2005 press conference, he was clearly angered at the idea posed by one questioner that he sought 'unchecked power', pointing out that he had consulted Congress a great deal. But 'consultation' is a difficult idea to define. Does it mean 'seeking opinions before making a decision' or merely 'listening to opinions after a decision has in essence been made'? There were many people in the Bush administration who believed that Congress's role is a subsidiary one when it comes to matters of national defence and security. 'The Constitution's intent when we're under attack from outside is to place maximum power in the president,' said William P. Barr, who was attorney-general to the first President Bush. With both houses of Congress under Republican control, many lawmakers were prepared to go along with this. 'Defending the country is pre-eminently an executive function,' said Republican congressman Tom Cole of Oklahoma. 'He is commander-in-chief, and you have to move with speed and dispatch.'

Thus, the move under George W. Bush towards the rebirth of the imperial presidency may have been more of a joint operation by the President and Congress than some coup d'état by the White House. 'It's not just the president pushing for more power,' said James Thurber, director of the Center for Congressional and Presidential Studies at American University; 'the Congress has not done its job of careful evaluation of giving the president more power post-9/11.'

But during the second Bush term, there were signs that this state of affairs was changing. Congressional opposition to the President's use of unauthorised phone-tapping and Congress's refusal to permanently extend the 2001 Patriot Act and its banning of 'cruel, inhuman or degrading' treatment of detainees in US custody anywhere in the world against the express wishes of the White House were seen as rebuffs to the power of the Bush administration. There were also a number of rebuffs to executive power handed down by the Supreme Court in such cases as *Hamdan* v. *Rumsfeld* (2006) and *Boumediene* v. *Bush* (2008).

However, not all scholars saw the George W. Bush White House as the imperial presidency reborn. To writer Sam Tanenhaus, Bush was not imperial, merely presidential.

Conclusions

The concept of the 'imperial presidency' offers something for everyone. It depends what people mean by it. In Lewis Carroll's *Alice Through the Looking-Glass*, Humpty Dumpty claims that 'when I use a word, it means just what I choose it to mean'. Many writers on the presidency have opted for the Humpty Dumpty theory of language when it comes to the 'imperial presidency.'

It is my view that, although Schlesinger's views are a useful opener for a discussion of presidential power, the concept of the 'imperial presidency' is flawed. In his memoirs, Richard Nixon stated that he believed that:

> The 'imperial presidency' was a straw man created by defensive congressmen and disillusioned liberals who in the days of FDR and John Kennedy had idolised the ideal of a strong presidency. Now they had a strong president who was a Republican — and Richard Nixon at that — they were having second thoughts.

In *The President of the United States* (1990), British academic David Mervin stated his belief that the concept of the imperial presidency 'was always something of a cliché', as it 'summons up images of the president as an emperor, a supreme sovereign authority, a master of all he surveys', which is clearly not the case.

In the *Wall Street Journal* of 27 December 2002, Sam Tanenhaus wrote an editorial entitled: 'Imperial? No, Presidential. Bush is no "Caesar"'. This is an appropriate piece with which to begin drawing our discussion together, because Tanenhaus illustrates in this article some of the problems associated with the whole imperial presidency debate — most of it comes down to looseness of terminology. Tanenhaus concludes:

> The imperial presidency is not a useful idea. It is an epithet, dredged up whenever a president combines strength with imagination. Presidents are, in sum, leaders not rulers — which means, of course, they are not imperial at all.

Professor Richard Davies of the University of Nevada, a prolific writer on past presidencies, was very near the mark when he stated that 'whether Bush is exhibiting an imperial presidential air is in the eye of the beholder'. The final word I leave to Dante Chinni, who rightly concludes that 'the president is as imperial as the Congress, the press and the public allow him to be'. In that sense the debate about the 'imperial presidency' in US politics parallels closely the debate in UK politics about the position of prime minister as an 'elective dictatorship', a term coined during the same decade.

Chapter 4

Task 4.1

Read the following extracts by Sam Tanenhaus and Arthur M. Schlesinger, and then answer the questions that follow.

Source A

The political performance of George W. Bush since September 11 2001 has left many marvelling at the discipline and efficiency of the president and his advisers. Together they 'have made the White House a power centre in ways that I haven't seen in a long, long time — all the way back to Lyndon Johnson,' said Robert Strauss, the former Democratic Party chairman and perennial adviser to presidents. Others are less impressed than alarmed by what they see as Mr Bush's flexing of executive muscle, overpowering the legislative and judicial branches.

Distrust of the 'imperial presidency' is a venerable tradition that dates back to our nation's beginnings. The Founders, keeping the example of George III firmly in mind, took every precaution to ensure that the new Republic would breed no home-grown tyrants. They envisioned a head of state who would 'preside' rather than rule.

But the current notion of the 'imperial presidency' is rooted not in the traditional fear of incipient monarchism but in its opposite, an almost cult-like fascination with executive power. Arthur Schlesinger, whose book *The Imperial Presidency* popularised the term, first made his reputation as a chronicler of two powerful presidents, Andrew Jackson and Franklin D. Roosevelt. Only with the advent of leaders uncongenial to liberal commentators did the frightening image of the 'imperial presidency' take hold.

First there was Lyndon Johnson, who vowed to carry out the Kennedy agenda and did so effectively but unaesthetically. Gone was the attractive 'vigour' and 'vitality' [of the presidency]. In its place were LBJ's 'boundless power appetite and ruthless ambition', in the words of Theodore White.

More disturbing still was Richard Nixon. Nixon's 'imperial presidency' smacked of dictatorship with its 'all-purpose invocation of "national security", the insistence on executive secrecy, the withholding of information from Congress, the attempted intimidation of the press'.

Now it is Mr Bush's turn. He is accused of cynically invoking national security, of relying too heavily on a few trusted advisers, of defying world opinion even as he runs roughshod over Congress, the courts and the press. Never mind that he has repeatedly taken his case to the people, to legislators, to the United Nations.

The 'imperial presidency' is not a useful idea. It is an epithet, dredged up whenever a president combines strength with imagination. Presidents are, in sum, leaders not rulers — which means, of course, that they are not imperial at all.

Adapted from Sam Tanenhaus, 'Imperial? No, presidential. Bush is no "Caesar"', **www.opinionjournal.com**, 27 December 2002

Task 4.1 (continued)

Source B

The so-called American empire is in fact a feeble imitation of the Roman, British and French empires. And yet the American presidency has come to see itself in messianic terms as the appointed savior of a world whose unpredictable dangers call for rapid and incessant deployment of men, arms, and decisions behind a wall of secrecy. This view seems hard to reconcile with the American Constitution. The impact of 9/11 and of the overhanging terrorist threat gives more power than ever to the imperial presidency and places the separation of powers ordained by the Constitution under unprecedented, and at times unbearable, strain.

Arthur M. Schlesinger Jr, *War and the American Presidency* (Norton, 2005)

(a) Explain how Sam Tanenhaus arrives at the conclusion that '"the imperial presidency" is not a useful idea'.

(b) Explain what Tanenhaus means by saying 'presidents are...leaders not rulers'.

(c) Explain why Schlesinger thinks that 'the separation of powers [is] under unprecedented, and at times unbearable, strain'.

Guidance

(a) The key to answering this question comes in the second-last sentence: 'The "imperial presidency" is not a useful idea. *It is an epithet, dredged up whenever a president combines strength with imagination.*' If you're unsure, find out the meaning of 'epithet'. Then look back at the three previous paragraphs where Tanenhaus uses three different presidencies as examples of what he means.

(b) ● Think what the words 'lead' and 'rule' actually mean.
   ● Consider about whom we usually use the words.
   ● You might ask whether a prime minister in the UK 'leads' or 'rules'.

(c) The key to answering this question comes in the second sentence of the quotation. Think of issues in the presidency of George W. Bush to which Schlesinger's comments might apply.

Further reading

● Mervin, D. (1990) *Ronald Reagan and the American Presidency*, Longman.
● Mervin, D. (1993) *The President of the United States*, Harvester-Wheatsheaf.
● Milkis, S. and Nelson, M. (1999) *The American Presidency*, CQ Press.
● Rudalevige, A. (2005) *The New Imperial Presidency*, University of Michigan Press.
● Schlesinger, A. M. (1973) *The Imperial Presidency*, Deutsch.
● Schlesinger, A. M. (2005) *War and the American Presidency*, Norton.

What has changed in the presidency since the 1960s?

Nowadays, people sometimes ask one another: 'Where were you when you first heard the news of the events of 9/11?' For my generation, the question was: 'Where were you when you first heard President Kennedy had been shot?' The assassination was on 22 November 1963. I was a 13-year-old schoolboy at the time. It was 7 o'clock in the evening, and my parents were listening to the BBC Light Programme — today's Radio 2. The scheduled programme was *Radio Newsreel*, 15 minutes of extra detail on the day's top stories. There was an unscheduled silence after the signature tune followed by the announcement that news had just come in that President Kennedy had been shot in Dallas, Texas.

Those events took place almost 50 years ago. How and to what extent has the office of the US presidency changed in those almost 50 years? What if a reincarnated President Kennedy 'landed' in Washington today? What would he find had changed? And why have those changes come about? Is the office of the presidency stronger or weaker than when he left it in November 1963? What surprises would be in store for him — other than the obvious one, that the occupant of the Oval Office is an African-American!

The subsequent occupants

Since the death of JFK in 1963, there have been nine occupants of the Oval Office. No surprises there. In the 50 years *before* 1963, there were eight occupants (see Table 5.1). In each of these periods, only three presidents managed to complete two full terms: Woodrow Wilson, Franklin Roosevelt and Dwight Eisenhower in the earlier period, Ronald Reagan, Bill Clinton and George W. Bush in the later one.

The eight earlier occupants came from diverse political backgrounds: three from state governorships (Wilson, Coolidge and Roosevelt), two from the vice-presidency (Coolidge and Truman), three from the Senate (Harding, Truman and

Kennedy), one from the cabinet (Hoover) and one from the military (Eisenhower). By contrast, of the nine later occupants, four were ex-state governors (Carter, Reagan, Clinton and George W. Bush), four from the vice-presidency (Johnson, Nixon, Ford and George H. W. Bush) and one from the Senate (Obama), although both Johnson and Nixon had earlier served in the Senate.

Table 5.1 US presidents, 1913–63 and 1963–2009 compared

US presidents, 1913–63	US presidents, 1963–2009
Woodrow Wilson (1913–21)	Lyndon Johnson (1963–69)
Warren Harding (1921–23)	Richard Nixon (1969–74)
Calvin Coolidge (1923–29)	Gerald Ford (1974–77)
Herbert Hoover (1929–33)	Jimmy Carter (1977–81)
Franklin Roosevelt (1933–45)	Ronald Reagan (1981–89)
Harry Truman (1945–53)	George H. W. Bush (1989–93)
Dwight Eisenhower (1953–61)	Bill Clinton (1993–2001)
John Kennedy (1961–63)	George W. Bush (2001–09)
	Barack Obama (2009–)

In both periods the two major parties controlled the presidency for disproportionate periods of time. During the 1913–63 period, the Democrats had the upper hand by 30 years to the Republicans' 20 years. During the 1963–2013 period, the Republicans will have come out on top by 28 years to 22.

The people who came to the presidency in the post-Kennedy era would cause JFK some surprises. The list includes Richard Nixon, whom Kennedy had beaten in the 1960 election, and Gerald Ford, a junior member of the House of Representatives back in 1963. I suspect Ronald Reagan's is the only other name Kennedy would recognise — though he might want to know how a Hollywood actor became one of his successors. But then, he might also be curious to know how a peanut farmer from Georgia (Jimmy Carter) with absolutely no experience of Washington politics came to be president. And, of course, Barack Hussein Obama.

New presidential nominating procedure

One of the most profound changes in the presidency in the post-Kennedy era is in the procedures for nominating presidential candidates. Back in 1960, when

Senator John Kennedy was running for the Democratic Party's presidential nomination, there were just 16 presidential primaries and only 38% of the delegates to that year's National Party Convention were chosen in them. Most of the delegates who gathered at the party convention in Los Angeles that year were chosen, not through primaries, but through caucuses or, more likely, through state party conventions. These were the 'smoke-filled rooms' dominated by the 'party bosses' — the bigwigs of state and local politics. Nearly 70% of Democratic senators and 90% of Democratic governors were delegates at the convention. It was a highly centralised, closed, elitist system by which the party hierarchy chose the party's presidential candidate.

Indeed, the presidential primaries were so *unimportant* that many well-known candidates didn't even enter them. Some, like Senator Kennedy, entered just a few to show their popularity and vote-getting abilities in different states. So, for example, in 1960 Senator Kennedy entered the West Virginia primary to show that, as a Catholic, he could win votes in a heavily Protestant state. The whole nominating process was incredibly short. Kennedy had no difficulty at all in continuing as a senator from Massachusetts while running for the presidential nomination. He announced his presidential campaign a mere 66 days before the first primary in New Hampshire.

Senator Kennedy did not need to spend a lot of time fund-raising. Even allowing for inflationary changes, election campaigns were cheaper in the 1960s. The money was given largely by a few wealthy donors — the 'fat cats' — not by ordinary voters giving $100 here or $250 there. Contrast all that with the current system of selecting presidential candidates and of campaign finance.

Back in the 1960s the national party conventions still played a significant role in the choosing of presidential candidates. With so few delegates chosen in the primaries, most of them came to the conventions uncommitted and willing to make up their mind in the convention hall. Conventions were therefore often highly unpredictable — and therefore rather interesting — affairs. As a result, the media paid a lot of attention to them and covered them from start to finish. For example, in 1968, NBC News devoted 23 hours to the coverage of each national party convention; by 2008, it gave just 4 hours to each convention.

Changing the way the choosing is done is likely to change the kind of people who get chosen. In the 1960s, the presidential candidates of the major parties were likely to be Washington insiders — a US senator or vice-president — but by two or three decades later, they were much more likely to be Washington outsiders, such as a state governor. As Table 5.2 shows, the change seemed to take effect in the mid-1970s. Five of the six presidents between 1945 and 1977 were Washington insiders — former senators, House members and vice-presidents. Only one of the six presidents since 1977 — George H. W. Bush — could truly be described as a Washington insider. Four of them had served only as state governors and so had no Washington experience at all. Barack Obama had served in the Senate a mere 4 years before becoming president.

| Table 5.2 | **Previous political experience of presidents, 1945–2009** |

Dates	President	Previous political experience
1945–53	Harry Truman	Senator, vice-president
1953–61	Dwight Eisenhower	None
1961–63	John Kennedy	House of Representatives, senator
1963–69	Lyndon Johnson	House of Representatives, senator, vice-president
1969–74	Richard Nixon	House of Representatives, senator, vice-president
1974–77	Gerald Ford	House of Representatives, vice-president
1977–81	Jimmy Carter	State governor
1981–89	Ronald Reagan	State governor
1989–93	George H. W. Bush	House of Representatives, vice-president
1993–2001	Bill Clinton	State governor
2001–09	George W. Bush	State governor
2009–	Barack Obama	Senator

Another change that John Kennedy might notice about the nine men who have succeeded him in the Oval Office is that five of them had some connection with the South, while only one was from the northern tier of states like him — Barack Obama of Illinois. Johnson (Texas), Carter (Georgia), Clinton (Arkansas) and George W. Bush (Texas) were all Southerners, and George H. W. Bush had served in the House of Representatives in the late 1960s from a Texas district. Of the other three presidents, two were Westerners (Nixon and Reagan, both from California) and one (Ford) was from the Midwest (Michigan). The only other candidates from the northern tier of states who featured in presidential elections were all losers, such as Michael Dukakis (1988) and John Kerry (2004) — both from Kennedy's home state of Massachusetts.

Changes in the White House

Were JFK to arrive at the White House little would have changed, at least on the surface, from the November day in 1963 when he and his wife left it for the last time for that fateful trip to Texas. He might notice that traffic no longer trundles past the front gate on Pennsylvania Avenue — a change brought about by security fears. The Oklahoma City bombing in 1995 brought about the street closure — a temporary move that has been made permanent.

Inside the building, too, the rooms are almost unchanged, other than in furnishings and colour schemes. But, organisation-ally, the White House is a much changed place. In Kennedy's day there was no White House press room with podium and permanent seating for the White House press pool. Back in the 1960s, the press were left to loiter on the driveway in all weathers,

The White House

invited into the White House only for big-ticket occasions. There was no daily press briefing. The briefing reflects another change — the coming of the 24-hour news channels and the need for the White House to constantly feed the rapacious appetite of Fox News, CNN and the like.

Kennedy would be familiar with the Executive Office of the President (EXOP), but nowadays it's a much expanded institution. He would recognise the National Security Council and the Council of Economic Advisors, but very little else. There would be quite a lot of explaining to do before Kennedy made sense of such EXOP offices as the Office on National AIDS Policy and the Office of Homeland Security. And what would the first Catholic president make of an Office of Faith-Based and Community Initiatives?

If Kennedy went to a cabinet meeting there would be more explaining to do. When JFK held his all-too-rare cabinet meetings, there were just ten depart-mental heads around the table. Now there are 15. We would have to explain the arrival of cabinet members dealing with Housing and Urban Development (1965), Transportation (1966), Energy (1977), Education (1979), Veterans' Affairs (1989) and Homeland Security (2002). One department represented at the cabinet table in Kennedy's day — the Post Office — has disappeared: it became a public corporation in 1970. With six new policy areas represented at cabinet level, Kennedy would find cabinet meetings far more diverse than the ones he remembered.

Presidential scandal leads to changed attitudes

It's not just institutional changes that have occurred in the presidency. There are attitudinal changes, too, especially among those outside the White House towards its occupant. Those 'outside' include Congress, the media and the US public. Vietnam, Watergate, Iran–Contra and Monica Lewinsky have all taken their toll on the office of the presidency. Although some Oval Office occupants have tried to refurbish the tarnished office — notably Jimmy Carter and George W. Bush — there has been a loss of awe and respect in terms of the public's perception of the presidency.

Here is Congressman Tom Foley, a leading Democrat congressman, talking as early as the 1980s:

> I think there's a great deal of loss of innocence about the presidency that stemmed from Watergate. Americans — both members of Congress and the general public — had always treated the presidency with a much different attitude than they had treated any other political office in America. For the presidency there was a special respect that was reserved. To some extent, the Watergate crisis sullied that respect and although there is now a high regard for most presidents as individuals, the presidency itself has never quite had the dimension it had before. It's now easier to criticise the president, even in foreign affairs, a little easier to ridicule occasionally alleged incompetence, than it was before. So there's been a bit of a scaling down of the presidential office and I think that is unfortunate in a way because our system doesn't work too well without a strong presidency.

Those words have hardly dated in the past 20 years or so. Both Bill Clinton and George W. Bush would recognise that 'it's now easier to criticise the president, even in foreign affairs' and that it's easier to ridicule him. If in doubt, take a browse through a website such as www.rushlimbaugh.com.

The media and the presidency

This leads us to another significant change that has affected the presidency during the past almost 50 years — the role of the media in US politics in general and the presidency in particular.

In Kennedy's day the media were dominated by the terrestrial television networks — ABC, CBS and NBC. This was the beginning of the heyday of the 6.30 p.m. news programmes with such anchors as David Brinkley and Walter Cronkite — 'the most trusted man in America'. Poor President Johnson was heard to lament: 'I can't compete with Walter Cronkite. He knows television and he's a star.' But at this time the media were mostly deferential. The president was given the benefit of the doubt. No reports of shenanigans at the White House during the Kennedy years — and we now know there were plenty of them.

Kennedy was elected in 1960 — the first truly made-for-television election. It was the televised debates between Senator Kennedy and Vice-President Nixon that really wedded television to the presidency — for better or worse. Kennedy's White House was made for television — a charming wife, a young family and a telegenic president who was good at performing for the cameras. According to presidential scholar Forrest McDonald, 'being president had become full-time show business' (*The American Presidency*, 1994).

But Vietnam and Watergate changed all that. A new breed of more aggressive reporter arrived on the screens. Sam Donaldson of *ABC News* now shouted questions at President Reagan across the White House lawn in a much less dignified manner than the one adopted by the likes of the cuddly Mr Cronkite. Under the Nixon administration, the relationship between the White House and the media was badly strained. A number of press folk appeared on the infamous White House 'enemies list', and Vice-President Agnew famously lambasted the media as both 'an effete corps of impudent snobs' and 'nattering nabobs of negativism'. Things had moved a long way from the honeymoon period of the Kennedy years.

However, presidents who were adept at handling the media — Ronald Reagan immediately comes to mind — were able to turn even this more aggressive and less forgiving attitude of the media to their own advantage. Donaldson later admitted to getting hundreds of letters from angry viewers, who berated him for what they saw as rudely shouting questions at the President from across the White House lawn. Dinesh D'Souza, writing in his insightful biography of Reagan (*Ronald Reagan: How an Ordinary Man Became an Extraordinary Leader*, 1997), reports that the general sentiment of the letters Donaldson received was 'Lay off the President. Give the man a break.' But Donaldson continued to yell his questions as the Reagan White House continued to deny him, and other White House correspondents, access to the President.

What Donaldson never cottoned on to was that the White House was deliberately keeping him and other media folk away from the President, thus forcing them to look rude and irritable, because:

> Reagan and his handlers wanted the American people to see the image of a president being harassed by the media. Donaldson never understood the degree to which he was playing a part in Reagan's script.

The 1980s proved to be the high-water mark for the likes of Sam Donaldson and Dan Rather. The 'old media' — dominated by print journalism and terrestrial television — were about to give way to the 'new media' of 24-hour cable television, the internet and 'bloggers'. Increasingly, younger Americans deserted the evening television news slots to watch CNN or Fox News or to visit their favourite websites.

According to Cronin and Genovese (*The Paradox of the American Presidency*, 2004), the media have turned the president into a celebrity-in-chief. The 24-hour news networks behave like prehistoric monsters, whose appetite for news, gossip, speculation and instant analysis is well-nigh insatiable. Television has become a crucial medium between the White House and people. No president can afford to neglect it. The George W. Bush White House, faced with mounting media and public criticism over its slow response to Hurricane Katrina in September 2005, resorted to live daily press briefings on the rescue effort.

Kennedy would doubtless be pleased with the way the medium that he loved and exploited so well has advanced its grip on the presidency. But whether those who invented the presidency would be as pleased is debatable. They feared that linking the presidency too closely to the public might undermine deliberation and reason. On this count, they would have reason to think that their fears were well founded.

Changes in the federal bureaucracy

The post-Kennedy years have witnessed a huge increase in the size and scope of the federal bureaucracy. Since Kennedy's days, six new executive departments have been created within the federal bureaucracy. Most of these policy areas were the concern of the federal government in Kennedy's days, but were not sufficiently important to warrant an executive department devoted to them. Housing and veterans' affairs, for example, were overseen by executive agencies. Education was overseen by the sprawling department of Health, Education and Welfare (HEW), formed in 1953 but separated in the late 1970s into the two separate departments of Health and Human Services (HHS) and Education. What now makes up the Department of Homeland Security was scattered throughout other departments and agencies.

Despite this 'growth' in the federal bureaucracy in terms of the number of executive departments, the size in terms of personnel has changed hardly at all since the days of President Kennedy. The total number of civilian federal government employees in 1960 — the year of Kennedy's election to the presidency — was 2.2 million. Today it is around 2.7 million.

What Kennedy would notice almost 50 years on is the look of those employees. To use a phrase much loved by Bill Clinton, the federal civil service now 'looks [more] like America' than it did 40 years ago. In 1960, the federal bureaucracy was 75% male. Today men account for 57% of federal civil servants. In 1960, the federal government wasn't even keeping statistics on the ethnic mix of civil servants. Kennedy himself voiced disapproval of the overwhelming white look of the government he inherited in 1961. By 2006, only 68% of the civil service was white — roughly in line with US society as a whole.

Changes in Congress

We could now walk President Kennedy the mile up Pennsylvania Avenue to Capitol Hill, to consider the changes in Congress that have affected the operation of the presidency. The walk itself would prompt some surprises. Mr Kennedy commented on the dowdiness of the USA's Main Street as he drove down it in his inaugural parade on 20 January 1961. As a result he set up a redevelopment commission, assigned with the task of smartening up this high-profile mile. And

Pennsylvania Avenue

what an impressive job they did. The old, dowdy buildings have been swept away and — mostly — graceful architecture has taken their place. Some of the dowdiness was renovated, rather than replaced — most notably the magnificent Willard Hotel, restored now to its early-twentieth-century grandeur. Some eyesores appeared, in particular the J. Edgar Hoover Building — headquarters of the FBI.

But on Capitol Hill, at least architecturally, little has changed. True, the House and Senate office buildings either side of Capitol Hill have grown in size. And there's the new Visitors' Center being built underneath the east front — the setting for Kennedy's famous inaugural speech (that centre is another reminder in this city of the effects of 9/11 and the need for greater security). Inside the Capitol, though, Kennedy would feel very much at home. Remember, Kennedy was far longer on Capitol Hill than in the White House. He spent 14 years in Congress — 6 in the House and 8 in the Senate — compared with under 3 years in the White House.

Congress now is very different from the one in which Kennedy served — and we will consider here the four changes in Congress that have most impacted upon the occupants of the White House.

First, Congress is a more fragmented institution than it was in the 1960s, and power in Congress is more diffuse. At the time of Eisenhower, Kennedy and Johnson (the 1950s and 1960s), Congress was run by a powerful few. Nowadays, in the words of Professor Anthony King, Congress is run not by the powerful few but by 'the considerably less powerful many'. Forty years ago, those who chaired the standing committees were extremely powerful. Phrases such as 'Kings of the Hill' and 'the Lords Proprietors of the Congress' were used to describe them. Get their agreement for a bill to be passed, a nomination to be confirmed or a treaty to be ratified, and it was done. Nowadays, presidents must do deals with hundreds of individual members of Congress. That makes the president's job far more difficult. In another memorable phrased coined by Professor King, the president these days often finds trying to work with Congress a frustrating business — 'It's rather like trying to sew buttons on a custard pie'.

Second, Congress is nowadays frequently controlled by the party not in control of the White House. We call this 'divided government'. For 37 of the 47 years up to Kennedy's death, the president and the majority of both houses of Congress were of the same party (see Table 5.3). In the 47 years after his death, the president and the majority of both houses of Congress were of the same party for only 17 years (Table 5.4), making the president's job difficult when it came to getting things done with Congress.

Table 5.3 **Party control of presidency and Congress, 1917–63**

Years	President	Party	Majority in Senate	Majority in House
1917–18	Wilson	D	D	R
1919–20	Wilson	D	R	D
1921–22	Harding	R	R	D
1923–24	Coolidge	R	R	R
1925–26	Coolidge	R	R	R
1927–28	Coolidge	R	R	R
1929–30	Hoover	R	R	R
1931–32	Hoover	R	R	R
1933–34	Roosevelt	D	D	D
1935–36	Roosevelt	D	D	D
1937–38	Roosevelt	D	D	D
1939–40	Roosevelt	D	D	D
1941–42	Roosevelt	D	D	D
1943–44	Roosevelt	D	D	D

Years	President	Party	Majority in Senate	Majority in House
1945–46	**Roosevelt/Truman**	**D**	**D**	**D**
1947–48	Truman	D	R	R
1949–50	**Truman**	**D**	**D**	**D**
1951–52	**Truman**	**D**	**D**	**D**
1953–54	**Eisenhower**	**R**	**R**	**R**
1955–56	Eisenhower	R	D	D
1957–58	Eisenhower	R	D	D
1959–60	Eisenhower	R	D	D
1961–62	**Kennedy**	**D**	**D**	**D**
1963	**Kennedy**	**D**	**D**	**D**

[Bold indicates one-party control of presidency and Congress]

Third, Congress has become a more assertive and powerful institution than it was 40 years ago. A number of factors have led to this resurgence of congressional authority. The most obvious is the Watergate affair, which resulted in the resignation of President Nixon because he no longer had the support of Congress. Nixon admitted as much in his resignation speech on 8 August 1974:

> Throughout the long and difficult period of Watergate, I have felt it was my duty to persevere, to make every possible effort to complete the term of office to which you elected me. In the past few days, however, it has become evident to me *that I no longer have a strong enough political base in the Congress to justify continuing that effort...* Therefore, I shall resign the presidency effective at noon tomorrow [my italics].

That Congress had forced a president from office, without even resorting to the full process of impeachment, would forever change the relationship between the two institutions.

Table 5.4 **Party control of presidency and Congress, 1964–2010**

Years	President	Party	Majority in Senate	Majority in House
1964	**Johnson**	**D**	**D**	**D**
1965–66	**Johnson**	**D**	**D**	**D**
1967–68	**Johnson**	**D**	**D**	**D**
1969–70	Nixon	R	D	D
1971–72	Nixon	R	D	D
1973–74	Nixon/Ford	R	D	D

Years	President	Party	Majority in Senate	Majority in House
1975–76	Ford	R	D	D
1977–78	**Carter**	**D**	**D**	**D**
1979–80	**Carter**	**D**	**D**	**D**
1981–82	Reagan	R	R	D
1983–84	Reagan	R	R	D
1985–86	Reagan	R	R	D
1987–88	Reagan	R	D	D
1989–90	Bush (41)	R	D	D
1991–92	Bush (41)	R	D	D
1993–94	**Clinton**	**D**	**D**	**D**
1995–96	Clinton	D	R	R
1997–98	Clinton	D	R	R
1999–2000	Clinton	D	R	R
2001–02	Bush (43)	R	R/D	R
2003–04	**Bush (43)**	**R**	**R**	R
2005–06	**Bush (43)**	**R**	**R**	**R**
2007–08	Bush (43)	R	D	D
2009–10	**Obama**	**D**	**D**	**D**

[Bold indicates one-party control of presidency and Congress]

Finally, Congress has become more partisan. The causes for this rise in partisanship are too numerous to detail here, but it is enough to mention two. First, the shift of the Southern conservatives from the Democrats to the Republicans has made both major parties more ideologically cohesive — the Democrats more liberal, the Republicans more conservative. Second, a number of the post-Kennedy presidents have been pretty divisive characters — Nixon, Clinton and George W. Bush come to mind — and they account for almost half of those years. Remember, too, that Nixon was forced to resign and Clinton was impeached by the House and tried — though found not guilty — by the Senate. Almost gone are the days when presidents could build bipartisan coalitions in Congress. Even as recently as the 1980s, Ronald Reagan governed successfully despite the Democrats controlling the House of Representatives, by appealing to Southern conservative Democrats to support his tax-cutting and

Richard Nixon

morally conservative programme. In the 1990s, if Bill Clinton tried to do deals with so-called moderate Republicans, he found that there weren't many of them left. Likewise, George W. Bush looked in vain for those conservative Democrats. They had already defected to his party. In the year Kennedy died, the Democratic Party held 95 of the 106 Southern House seats and all 22 of the Southern Senate seats. Forty years later, in 2003, the Democrats held only 55 of the 131 House seats and only 9 of the 22 Senate seats.

Conclusions

In the nearly 50 years since President Kennedy was assassinated, American politics has undergone profound changes, many of them brought about by the convulsive events of these years. Indeed, the office of the American presidency looks pretty resilient when one considers what it has survived — Kennedy's assassination, anti-Vietnam War protests, Nixon's resignation, the Cold War, the 'new media', Clinton's impeachment and 9/11.

As a result of these events, American politics is now more open to view and more open to criticism. But rather as with Britain's royal family, the more we let in the light, the less we may like what we see. Kennedy benefited from an aura of deference towards the office that modern presidents just don't have. Washington is now a more complicated and difficult place in which to do business than it was in the days of President Kennedy.

And given that the prevailing issues that have most affected the presidency — the 24-hour news media, the threats from terrorism — are not about to go away, one can envisage that the situation for presidents in another 50 years' time might be even more difficult. That said, the election of less divisive characters as president and ones with more Washington experience than most recent office-holders have had, and a continuation of the trend towards united, rather than divided, control of the White House and Congress, could see this prediction looking unnecessarily bleak. The office has survived much since its inception. It will probably survive a lot more.

Task 5.1

Read Source A and answer the questions that follow.

Source A

The presidency changes from season to season, occupant to occupant, issue to issue. We may never unravel most of the paradoxes of the American presidency. Strong individuals in demanding times, with the support of Congress and the public,

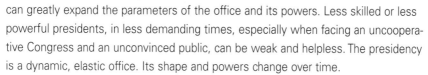

Task 5.1 (continued)

can greatly expand the parameters of the office and its powers. Less skilled or less powerful presidents, in less demanding times, especially when facing an uncooperative Congress and an unconvinced public, can be weak and helpless. The presidency is a dynamic, elastic office. Its shape and powers change over time.

Perhaps, then, we should celebrate the work of the inventors of this unique office. Is the genius of the framers that they created an office capable of adapting to the needs and demands of an ever-changing world? They invented an office just ambiguous enough to adapt, yet not so loose and undefined that it could easily overwhelm the delicate balance of the separation of powers.

The office of the presidency has an enormous, larger-than-life quality. In spite of the dramatic ups and downs of the office in the past 50 years, it does seem to be, in Arthur Schlesinger's words, 'the indestructible institution'. It is at once the most powerful and the weakest executive office in the world. The great opportunity to do good is matched by the equally strong capacity to do great harm. The constitutional design of the office was left vague enough to give presidents an opportunity to shape and mould the office to conform, in part, to the needs of the time, the level of political opportunity, and the skills of each incumbent. But it was also an office encumbered by obstacle after obstacle.

Michael Genovese, *The Power of the American Presidency, 1789–2000* (2001)

(a) Explain why Genovese thinks that the inventors of the presidency — the framers of the Constitution — did such a good job in their devising of the US presidency.

(b) What 'dramatic ups and downs' can you think of that have affected the US presidency in the last 50 years?

Guidance

(a) The key to the answer lies in the last two sentences of the opening paragraph.

(b) If you need help with ideas for this look at the conclusions to this chapter. You may also go to **www.americanpresident.org** and click on 'Presidency in History'. Click on the date 1969 and you will find pages on the presidents from Richard Nixon to George W. Bush. Click on an image to select a president. Click on 'Key Events' and a time line will appear on the right side of the screen which you can scroll down.

Further reading

- Cronin, T. E. and Genovese, M. A. (2004) *The Paradoxes of the American Presidency*, Oxford University Press.
- Genovese, M. (2001) *The Power of the American Presidency, 1789–2000*, OUP.
- Pika, J. (2006) *The Politics of the Presidency*, CQ Press.

George W. Bush: success or failure?

'A pleasant man, without any qualifications for the office.' Assessing presidents is tricky. Is this quotation a fair assessment of the 43rd president, George W. Bush? Some would say 'yes' — though they might question the adjective 'pleasant'! But others would disagree. The trouble is, this comment was not made about the 43rd president, but the 32nd president — none other than Franklin D. Roosevelt, probably the most highly regarded president of the twentieth century. Whether a president is a success or a failure is not always clear upon his leaving office. So all we can do at this time is to offer an initial assessment of the George W. Bush presidency rather than a final word.

Bush's successes

While in Washington DC towards the close of the Clinton presidency, I remember going into the large Borders bookstore on L Street and seeing on the 'newly published' table a book with (something like) the title *Bill Clinton's Greatest Political Achievements*. Not being a great admirer of Bill, I was surprised that it was such a thick book. I picked up a copy to scan the contents. Every page was blank! Some might think that a book on George W. Bush's successes ought to be similarly empty, but I have six successes to analyse.

George W. Bush

(1) He served two full consecutive terms

George W. Bush became president on 20 January 2001 and left office on 20 January 2009, serving two full and consecutive 4-year terms. This may not in itself appear much of an achievement. However, in the 132 years between 1877 and 2009 there were 24 presidents, and only 6 of these 24 served two full consecutive terms: Democrats Woodrow Wilson, FDR and Bill Clinton, and Republicans Dwight Eisenhower, Ronald Reagan and George W. Bush.

(2) He kept the country safe after 9/11

Bush's presidency was in its 234th day when the planes slammed into the World Trade Center in New York City and the Pentagon in Washington DC, and the White House Chief of Staff Andrew Card whispered in the President's ear as he sat reading to a class of 7-year-olds in Sarasota, Florida: 'America is under attack.' Addressing a joint session of Congress 9 days later, the President promised:

> We will direct every resource at our command to the disruption of the global terror network. I will not yield, I will not rest, I will not relent in waging this struggle for freedom and security for the American people.

In that moment and with these sentences, the standard for the Bush presidency was set: to protect Americans from another attack on their homeland — another 9/11 — as well as to hit Islamist terrorists and their sponsors abroad. In the over 7 years of Bush's presidency that followed, US law enforcement and intelligence agencies foiled numerous terrorist attempts within the United States, such as one to blow up the Brooklyn Bridge in New York City. In his farewell address to the nation (15 January 2009), the President reminded Americans of those fears of further attacks, and said of his administration's continued vigilance:

> As the years passed, most Americans were able to return to life much as it had been before 9/11. But I never did. Every morning, I received a briefing on the threats to our nation. And I vowed to do everything in my power to keep us safe.

The trouble, however, is that Bush's achievement is that nothing happened, and that those who are protected from danger often conclude that there was no danger.

(3) Legislative successes

Given that George W. Bush had his own party in control of Congress for the majority of his presidency, one would expect his legislative successes to have been relatively substantial. But even Bush's supporters would be pushed to come

up with a lengthy list. His principal successes came early on with the No Child Left Behind (NCLB) Act and the $1.35 trillion tax cut — both in 2001. There was a further $350 billion tax cut in 2003.

In his successes in Congress, Bush showed the art of compromise — an attribute which was often lacking in other areas of his presidency. Bush had the knack of laying out what he wanted, compromising — even giving in — and then claiming victory. With the NCLB Act, he got the late Democrat senator Edward Kennedy — a noted liberal — on board by dropping his insistence on school vouchers. He managed to claim credit for the McCain–Feingold Bipartisan Campaign Reform Act of 2002 despite having opposed it during its passage through Congress. It was much the same when it came to reorganising the intelligence agencies after 9/11. Initially, Bush wanted to create an office within the Executive Office of the President to oversee homeland security. But recognising Congress's proposal to create a new executive department as the only plan that was going anywhere, Bush jumped on board, fought for it, won and claimed the credit.

It was much the same when it came to the 2003 tax cut. The President proposed a $726 billion tax cut and derided the $350 billion version passed by the Senate. But when the House agreed to the Senate's version, suddenly Bush was claiming as a victory the plan he had only weeks before dismissed as a failure. 'Sometime I get everything I want, and sometimes I don't,' the President told lawmakers at a private meeting.

(4) Regime change

> Thanks to Mr Bush, more than 55 million people today, in Afghanistan and Iraq, are freed from brutal dictatorships — the Taliban in Afghanistan, and Saddam Hussein's regime in Iraq.

So wrote the *Wall Street Journal* in its editorial the day before President Bush left office in January 2009. The iconic photograph of the toppling of the statue of Saddam Hussein in Baghdad will be one of the abiding memories of the Bush presidency. Of course, one is not suggesting that the military operations in Afghanistan and Iraq were unvarnished successes, and we shall return to this matter later when we consider Bush's failures.

George W. Bush's legacy in these two states is still to be decided. Will Iraq become a stable, pro-Western democracy amidst the Arab world, or will it stagger from one crisis to another, beset by sectarian violence? Certainly Bush may stand a better chance of being judged a successful president on Iraq following his courageous decision to send an additional 30,000 troops there in his final 2 years, against intense partisan opposition, in what became known as the Surge.

(5) Supreme Court appointments

Bush's most enduring success — at least in the eyes of conservatives — may well turn out to be his appointments of John Roberts and Samuel Alito to the US Supreme Court. Their relative youthfulness and their life tenure mean that both these Bush appointees could still be on the court in 2030, maybe even 2040. Both have so far proved to be solid conservatives.

Although John Roberts was appointed as Chief Justice — with the post's attendant importance — it will probably be the appointment of Samuel Alito which will turn out to Bush's biggest success. In replacing William Rehnquist with John Roberts, the President merely replaced one conservative with another. But in replacing Sandra Day O'Connor with Samuel Alito, there is much evidence already to suggest that he replaced a moderate 'swing' justice with a conservative one. Alito's appointment has potentially swung the court to the right, much to the pleasure of Bush's supporters.

(6) Restored dignity to the Oval Office

When Governor George W. Bush pledged during his 2000 campaign to 'restore dignity to the Oval Office', everyone knew exactly what he meant. He didn't have to hold up a picture of his finger-wagging, red-faced predecessor at the White House podium saying, 'I did not have sexual relations with that woman — Ms Lewinsky.' When newsreel film was shown in US cinemas in the late 1990s showing President Clinton comforting female disaster victims with a perfectly innocent and proper presidential embrace, audiences sniggered. There was never any danger of them doing so when his successor was frequently filmed in an identical pose after 9/11.

Bush's failures

That George W. Bush's presidency was beset by numerous failures is hardly in doubt. For proof one need only look at the downward trajectory of his approval ratings from 2003 to 2009. From an approval rating immediately after 9/11 of over 90 percent, Bush's approval rating fell away to the 20 percent range through much of his final year. We shall consider six failures which partly accounted for this decline in public esteem.

(1) Foreign policy failures

Where to start? The list of foreign policy failures is extensive: not finding weapons of mass destruction in Iraq; going into Iraq with inadequate manpower; expecting

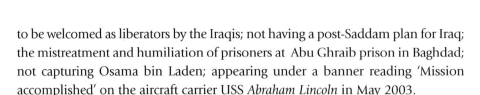

to be welcomed as liberators by the Iraqis; not having a post-Saddam plan for Iraq; the mistreatment and humiliation of prisoners at Abu Ghraib prison in Baghdad; not capturing Osama bin Laden; appearing under a banner reading 'Mission accomplished' on the aircraft carrier USS *Abraham Lincoln* in May 2003.

As the President faced his final press conference on 12 January 2009, he was still reluctant to describe many of these episodes as failures or mistakes. Asked, 'Do you think in retrospect that you have made any mistakes?' Mr Bush replied:

> I have often said that history will look back and determine the mistakes I made. Clearly putting 'Mission accomplished' on an aircraft carrier was a mistake. It sent the wrong message. Obviously some of my rhetoric has been a mistake . . . There have been disappointments. Abu Ghraib was a huge disappointment during the presidency. Not having [*sic.*] weapons of mass destruction was a significant disappointment. I don't know if you want to call these mistakes or not, but they were — things didn't go according to plan, let's put it that way.

(2) Civil liberty failures

Again, there's something of a list in terms of the Bush administration's failure to safeguard and protect civil rights and liberties, both of US citizens and those of countries where the USA was engaged in military action. The list would include: Guantánamo Bay; military tribunals; waterboarding; wiretapping; the Patriot Act. Some would add the names of Bush administration officials: Vice-President Dick Cheney and his chief of staff Lewis 'Scooter' Libby; Secretary of Defense Donald Rumsfeld; Attorney-General Alberto Gonzales.

The President had his knuckles rapped more than once by the United States Supreme Court for what it regarded as failures to safeguard civil liberties. In the 2004 case of *Rasul* v. *Bush*, the court by a margin of 6–3 struck down some important parts of the administration's legal policy regarding its war on terrorism in general and the detainees at Guantánamo Bay in particular. The court ruled that, contrary to the claims of the President, these detainees did have access to the United States federal courts to challenge their detention.

Two years later, in *Hamdan* v. *Rumsfeld*, the court declared unconstitutional the military commissions set up by Bush to try people at Guantánamo Bay. And in 2008, in *Boumediene* v. *Bush*, the court ruled that the procedures set up by the Bush administration following the *Hamdan* decision were inadequate to ensure that the detainees had their day in court. Justice Anthony Kennedy, for the court's five-member majority, scolded the President:

> The laws and the Constitution are designed to survive, and remain in force, in extraordinary times. Liberty and security can be reconciled.

And these failures in civil liberties caused significant problems for the way the United States was viewed abroad.

(3) Hurricane Katrina

George W. Bush's presidency, which had been transformed by a man-made disaster in September 2001, was transformed once more by a natural disaster in August 2005. The federal government in general, and the President in particular, failed to respond in a manner appropriate to the unfolding disaster which was Hurricane Katrina.

Hurricane Katrina made landfall in southeast Louisiana on 29 August 2005 as a Category 3 storm. It would be the costliest and one of the deadliest storms ever to hit the United States. Nearly 2,000 died from the storm and the flooding that resulted from the failure of the levees, which were meant to protect low-lying areas of New Orleans. The nearly 3,000 deaths on 9/11 just 4 years earlier had rallied the nation around their President. But the deaths from Hurricane Katrina led to a firestorm of criticism about the way the President handled the response to the crisis. That's not to say that the state and local officials were blameless, but in a disaster of this magnitude, people look to the federal government and to their president as organiser- and comforter-in-chief.

The President's failure to visit New Orleans after the disaster was a mistake. Instead he circled the city on Air Force One and was photographed peering out of a cabin window onto the disaster below. It was not the same as seeing the President standing on top of the rubble of the World Trade Center, addressing rescuers through a bullhorn, as had been the case post-9/11. Now the President looked remote and unengaged. With pictures on television of the chaotic scenes in New Orleans, the President publicly praised the director of the Federal Emergency Management Agency, Michael Brown, in that now-infamous phrase: 'Brownie, you're doing a heck of a job.' Within days, Brown resigned amidst widespread public criticism of his — and the President's — handling of the disaster.

Bush did eventually make it to a deserted New Orleans, where in an eerily empty city he made his sort-of-acknowledgement of failure:

> It was not a normal hurricane, and the normal disaster relief system was not equal to it. When the federal government fails to meet such an obligation, I as president am responsible for the problem, and for the solution.

As Bush biographer Robert Draper (*Dead Certain*, 2007) commented:

> Blinking, one might have missed it — but there it was, the President owning up to his share of the blame.

(4) He alienated conservatives

Another failure of George W. Bush was to alienate his conservative Republican base. There was his profligate federal spending — increasing at a faster rate than under any president since Lyndon Johnson. Then there was Bush's refusal to wield the veto pen until the 66th month of his presidency, using only 11 regular vetoes and 1 pocket veto in his 8 years in the Oval Office. Conservatives wanted Bush to veto what they saw as wasteful spending by Congress. Then, towards the end of his presidency, there was Mr Bush doling out $700 billion of taxpayers' money in the Wall Street and bank bailout scheme.

Add to all this Mr Bush's nomination of Harriet Miers to the US Supreme Court. Conservatives were unconvinced that this virtually unknown lawyer was 'one of us'. The President tried to reassure them:

> I've known Harriet for more than a decade, I know her heart, I know her character.

But under a firestorm of criticism from his own side, the President allowed Miers to withdraw from the nomination. In her place, he nominated a true conservative, Judge Samuel Alito. But the damage was done.

(5) Budget deficits and economic collapse

On almost every economic indicator, the Bush years came up short. Unemployment rose from 4.2 percent in January 2001 to 7.2 percent in December 2008. The Dow Jones Industrial Average fell from 11,723 a week before Bush took office to 7,552 by mid-September 2008. A federal budget surplus of $120 billion in 2001 turned into a deficit of $420 billion by 2008. The national debt went through the roof; house prices fell through the floor. In 1980, during his first presidential campaign, Ronald Reagan liked to ask: 'Are you better off than you were 4 years ago?' The answer of most Americans back then was 'no'. They gave the same answer in 2008. When exit polls asked 2008 voters to describe the condition of the nation's economy, a mere 7 percent described it as excellent or good; 93 percent described is as not so good or poor. When asked, 'How worried are you that the current economic crisis will harm your family's finances over the next year?', 81 percent said they were worried. They judged George W. Bush's economic stewardship a failure.

(6) Personal failings

Finally, there are what I have chosen to call Bush's personal failings. In many ways, George W. Bush is a likable person: affable; possessing a good sense of humour; moral; a good role model; a committed Christian who practises what he preaches. But what some see as strengths, others see as weaknesses. To his admirers, Bush is supremely confident; to his critics, he is stubborn. To his admirers he is decisive; to his critics, he is arrogant. Furthermore, personal traits that were a strength in one situation turned into a weakness in another. The

Washington Post in its final editorial on President Bush (18 January 2009) two days before he left office, remarked:

> His certitude amid the crisis of September 11, 2001 helped galvanise the initial national response, including the toppling of the Taliban in Afghanistan. Alas, that same certitude led Mr Bush down many blind alleys and, in the worst moments, caused him to debase the country's moral currency.

According to John Dickerson and Karen Tumulty in *Time* magazine (1 December 2003):

> To some, the way Bush walks and talks and smiles is the body language of courage and self-assurance, and of someone who shares their values. But to others, it is the swagger and smirk that signals the certainty of the stubbornly simpleminded.

Bush liked to depict himself as 'the decider'. Just 7 months into his presidency — a fortnight before 9/11 — a pupil at an elementary school in his home town of Crawford, Texas, asked the President if it was 'hard to make decisions' as president. Bush replied:

> Not really. If you know what you believe, decisions come pretty easy. If you're one of those types of people that are always trying to figure out which way the wind is blowing, decision making can be difficult. But I know who I am. I know what I believe in, and I know where I want to lead this country.

White House speechwriter David Frum described Bush as 'relentlessly disciplined', yet also a man 'sometimes glib, even dogmatic; often incurious and as a result ill-informed; more conventional in his thinking than a leader should probably be'.

The Bush legacy

Bush's political effect on the Republican Party bordered on the disastrous. The Republicans won 9 fewer states — commanding 113 Electoral College votes — in 2008 than they did in 2004. Combining the 2006 and 2008 elections, they lost 14 seats in the Senate, 54 seats in the House and 6 state governorships. After the 2006 mid-term elections, Bush admitted that 'it was a thumping' as far as the Republicans were concerned. And in 2008, the Republicans nominated as their presidential candidate someone who was the most unlike Bush of all their potential nominees — John McCain — and who desperately tried to distance himself from his own party's incumbent president.

According to James Ceaser (*The Epic Journey*, 2009):

> George W. Bush was not on the ballot in 2008, but he might just as well have been. For according to [Obama strategists] David Axelrod and David Plouffe, all that was wrong with the United States could be summarised in one word: Bush.

What legacy have commentators and presidency-watchers ascribed to Bush? As we shall see in our final chapter, the 2009 C-SPAN presidential leadership survey posted him 36th out of the 42 presidents. His nearest post-war colleague was Richard Nixon (27th) and the only twentieth-century president below him was Warren Harding at 38th. That's quite damning.

Not all would agree. According to Bush biographer Robert Draper:

> The nation very much needed a president with [Mr Bush's] level of certitude, with that clarity of vision such that he could say, 'you're either for us or you're for the terrorists', someone who could bring forth from the public a great amount of pride in America and a great amount of determination.

Most commentators stress that the jury is still out on George W. Bush and that much depends on what happens regarding international terrorism and in Iraq in the coming decades. According to Professor George Edwards:

> If Iraq should turn into a stable democracy and a model for the Middle East, that will be a huge plus in his legacy… History will view this as a consequential presidency. George W. Bush was one who thought boldly and aimed explicitly to make a lasting impact.

But to discover what that impact will be and whether George W. Bush will ultimately be regarded as a success or a failure, we must await the judgement of history.

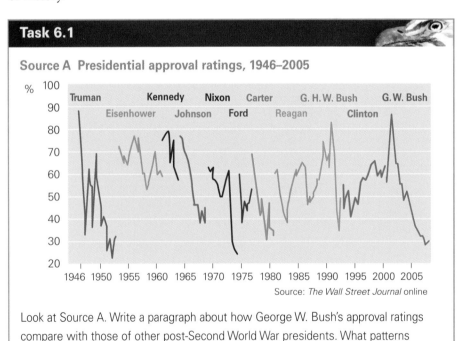

Task 6.1

Source A Presidential approval ratings, 1946–2005

Source: *The Wall Street Journal* online

Look at Source A. Write a paragraph about how George W. Bush's approval ratings compare with those of other post-Second World War presidents. What patterns emerge in the graphs of these 11 presidents?

Task 6.1 (continued)

Guidance

Compare the performances of the four two-term presidents — Eisenhower, Reagan, Clinton and George W. Bush. Compare approval ratings at the start and end of each presidency. The Gallup polling organisation website has graphs for each of these presidencies in much greater detail. Go to **www.gallup.com**, then under the 'Politics and Government' button click on 'Poll Topics: Topics A–Z'; under 'P', click on 'Presidential Approval Ratings: Gallup Historical Statistics and Trends'; click on 'page 2'.

Task 6.2

Source B Total deficits vs national debt increases

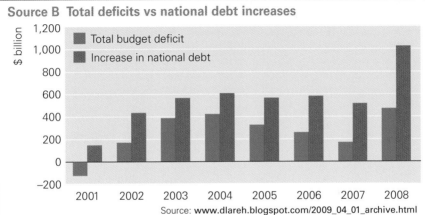

Source: www.dlareh.blogspot.com/2009_04_01_archive.html

Source C US house prices, 1988–2008

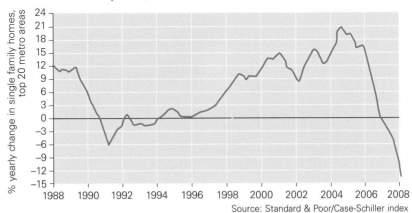

Source: Standard & Poor/Case-Schiller index

Look at Sources B and C. Write a paragraph explaining what these data show about the state of the federal budget surplus/deficit, the national debt and US house prices during the George W. Bush years.

Task 6.2 (continued)

Guidance

Clearly both sources show bad economic news. Try to assess the extent to which George W. Bush might be held accountable for each of these three economic indicators.

Further reading

- Bruni, F. (2002) *Ambling into History: The Unlikely Odyssey of George W. Bush*, HarperCollins.
- Cannon, L. and Cannon, C. (2008) *Reagan's Disciple: George W. Bush's Troubled Quest for a Presidential Legacy*, Public Affairs.
- Draper, R. (2007) *Dead Certain: The Presidency of George W. Bush*, Free Press.
- Frum, D. (2003) *The Right Man: An Inside Account of the Surprise Presidency of George W. Bush*, Weidenfeld and Nicolson.
- McClellan, S. (2008) *What Happened: Inside the Bush White House*, Public Affairs.
- Woodward, B. (2002) *Bush at War*, Simon and Schuster.
- Woodward, B. (2004) *Plan of Attack*, Simon and Schuster.
- Woodward, B. (2006) *State of Denial*, Simon and Schuster.
- Woodward, B. (2008) *The War Within*, Simon and Schuster.

What makes a good president?

In the first chapter we asked the question: 'What does anyone need to become president?' Here we are asking a different, though related, question. Some of the characteristics and qualities required to *become* president are also required to *be* a successful president, which is reassuring. It would, after all, be alarming to discover that there was no link at all between these two lists of qualities. So, in considering the qualities that help towards making a good — or, more accurately, effective or successful — president, we can take three of them as done and dusted: relevant policies, oratorical skills and organisational skills. These were fully considered in chapter 1. But we need to consider six other qualities: popularity; party control of Congress; an understanding of Washington politics; an understanding of international politics; moral authority; and an ability to persuade.

Obama on the campaign trail, 2008

Popularity

Some presidents *just* win elections — Jimmy Carter in 1976, for example. In that election, Carter polled just under 50.1% of the popular vote, while his opponent, President Gerald Ford, polled just over 48%. In the Electoral College it was 297–240. Some presidents, however, 'win big': Lyndon Johnson in 1964 and Ronald Reagan in 1984. Johnson won over 61% of the popular vote in 1964, and, in 1984, Reagan won 525 of the 538 Electoral College votes. Big wins ought to make a president's job easier, since they provide an overwhelming mandate from the people to carry out the president's programme. Lyndon Johnson and Ronald Reagan both, to some extent, benefited from big wins. Jimmy Carter found things tough going and lost his re-election bid 4 years later. Obama's 53% of the popular vote in 2008 was the highest percentage for any presidential candidate since 1988: not a big win, but bigger than had become usual.

Not that big wins are a guarantee of a successful presidency. Like Lyndon Johnson in 1964, Richard Nixon in 1972 also won 61% of the popular vote and won 520 Electoral College votes, but in under 2 years Nixon was forced to resign, his popularity having hit rock bottom as a result of the Watergate affair. What this shows is that, having won an election, presidents need to maintain their popularity in order to be successful. It was often said that Bill Clinton survived his impeachment in 1998 and trial by the Senate in 1999 because of his persistently high approval ratings. Within 8 months of being re-elected in 2004, George W. Bush's approval ratings had fallen below 40%.

Party control of Congress

A factor that often leads to presidential success is for the president's party to control both houses of Congress. Table 7.1 shows the 12 presidents who held office between 1933 and 2009 — from FDR to George W. Bush. They are ranked in order of 'success' as rated by the C-SPAN survey of presidential leadership conducted in 2009. Of the top four in the table, all enjoyed party control of both houses of Congress for part or all of their presidencies. Of the bottom five in the table, three never had their party in control of either house of Congress. The exceptions to the rule appear to be Eisenhower, Carter and George W. Bush. Eisenhower, despite controlling the House and Senate for only 2 of his 8 years, ranks 4/12. Carter, despite enjoying control of both houses throughout his 4-year term, ranks only 10/12, and George W. Bush, despite controlling both houses for a majority of his presidency, ranks 12/12.

| Table 7.1 | Presidential success and party control of Congress, 1933–2009 |

Rank	President	House controlled by same party?	Senate controlled by same party?
1	Franklin Roosevelt (D)	Yes	Yes
2	Harry Truman (D)	Part: 6/8	Part: 6/8
3	John Kennedy (D)	Yes	Yes
4	Dwight Eisenhower (R)	Part: 2/8	Part: 2/8
5	Ronald Reagan (R)	No	Part: 6/8
6	Lyndon Johnson (D)	Yes	Yes
7	Bill Clinton (D)	Part: 2/8	Part: 2/8
8	George H. W. Bush (R)	No	No
9	Gerald Ford (R)	No	No
10	Jimmy Carter (D)	Yes	Yes
11	Richard Nixon (R)	No	No
12	George W. Bush (R)	Part: 6/8	Part 4½/8

The job of the president in dealing with Congress is not made easy by the structure of US government. The decentralised nature of government in a federal system, the separation of powers and strict separation of personnel between the executive and the legislature, as well as the decentralised nature of US political parties, conspire to make the president detached from Congress. Whereas the UK prime minister is the elected leader of the largest party — usually the majority party — in the House of Commons, of which the prime minister and his or her government are also members, the US president is not really party leader at all and is physically excluded from the Congress, as are the other members of the president's administration. Hence, what the UK prime minister can achieve by 'hands-on' control, the US president must achieve by 'remote control'.

All this is no accident. It was the plan of the Founding Fathers. In his farewell address of 1796, President George Washington warned of the 'spirit of party' and warned that political parties would be 'the curse of the country'. Although political parties have developed in the two centuries since Washington's warnings, political changes in recent decades have made the president more remote both from the party and from Congress. Presidential candidates of the first two-thirds of the twentieth century were chosen largely by the party hierarchy — the party bosses. The party therefore felt that, once the president had been chosen and elected, the party had a vested interest in their success. Presidents such as Harry Truman (1945–53), Lyndon Johnson (1963–69) and

Richard Nixon (1969–74) were all congressional insiders. Since the 1970s, presidential candidates have been chosen not by the party but by ordinary voters in primaries and are therefore less likely to be drawn from among congressional insiders. Members of Congress, even from the president's party, no longer feel that there is a long-standing link between them and the president. Presidents such as Jimmy Carter, Bill Clinton and George W. Bush found it much harder to manage Congress as a result.

Consequently, Cronin and Genovese suggest that we might be moving to what they call 'a no-party presidency'. In *The Paradoxes of the American Presidency* (2004), they write:

> Parliamentary regimes such as Great Britain have strong disciplined parties, and the prime minister can rely on the party in Parliament to gain passage of his or her proposals. But in the United States, with weak, undisciplined parties, presidential power is more personalised. While parties matter in the United States, they do not matter as much as in Britain or other European democracies.

The president has few carrots to offer to encourage party discipline. The jobs that the president has to offer — membership of the cabinet, ambassadorships and so on — are rarely those that ambitious members of Congress aspire to. Neither does the president have many sticks to discourage mavericks. As a result, in most dealings with Congress, the president must be 'bargainer-in-chief', in the words of David Mervin.

An understanding of Washington politics

We suggested above that presidents of past decades — Truman, Johnson and Nixon — were often 'Washington insiders'. As a result, they had an intricate knowledge and understanding of how Washington works. But more recently, presidents have been drawn from the ranks of 'Washington outsiders'. Carter, Reagan, Clinton and the younger George Bush had no experience of Washington politics at all, and Obama's Washington experience was exceedingly limited. In the 32 years between 1945 and 1977, the White House was occupied for 24 years by someone who could be called a Washington insider. Only Eisenhower (1953–61) was a Washington outsider. But in the 34 years between 1977 and 2010, the White House will have been occupied by a Washington insider for only 4 years. Only George H. W. Bush (1989–93) was a Washington insider. It is the complete opposite.

One must therefore ask how recent — outsider — presidents gain an understanding of Washington politics other than by what one might call 'on-the-job training'. One way for such presidents to enhance their understanding of Washington politics is to ensure that senior members of their administration are drawn from the pool of Washington politicians. For some, this was done by choosing a vice-president who was a Washington insider. Carter, Clinton and Obama chose former senators — respectively Walter Mondale, Al Gore and Joe Biden. Reagan had George H. W. Bush, who had served in Washington in a number of capacities — congressman, Republican Party chairman, ambassador and CIA director. George W. Bush chose Dick Cheney — a former House minority whip and secretary of defense.

The post of White House chief of staff is another key position. George W. Bush chose Andrew Card, a consummate Washington insider, and Barack Obama chose Rahm Emanuel, a former Clinton White House staffer and then a member of Congress. Jimmy Carter fell badly in this regard, refusing even to appoint a chief of staff for much of his presidency and then appointing someone who, like himself, had no Washington experience at all. Clinton fell for the same mistake at the start of his first term but learned faster than Carter, appointing former House Budget Committee chairman Leon Panetta to the post in 1994.

Although neither came to the White House with experience of Washington politics, Jimmy Carter and George W. Bush offer a stark contrast in how critical it is to quickly develop an understanding of the way Washington works. Carter continually made missteps in this, from refusing the House speaker extra tickets for the inauguration, to sending a bill to members of Congress who attended a working breakfast at the White House. In contrast, one of George W. Bush's first gestures as president was to invite Senator Edward Kennedy and his wife for a candlelit dinner at the White House. Kennedy, a liberal Democrat, was the senior Democrat on the Senate Education Committee and Bush wanted to pass a flagship education reform bill through Congress in his first year.

An understanding of international politics

A president's effectiveness in international relations is often viewed separately from the success of his administration as a whole. No two presidents illustrate this more starkly than Lyndon Johnson and Richard Nixon. Johnson is generally rated highly as a president. The C-SPAN survey (2009) of presidential leadership

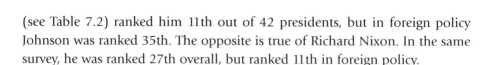

(see Table 7.2) ranked him 11th out of 42 presidents, but in foreign policy Johnson was ranked 35th. The opposite is true of Richard Nixon. In the same survey, he was ranked 27th overall, but ranked 11th in foreign policy.

Table 7.2 **The C-SPAN (2009) survey of presidential leadership**

Rank	President	Rank	President
1	Abraham Lincoln	22	Gerald Ford
2	George Washington	23	Ulysses Grant
3	Franklin D. Roosevelt	24	William Howard Taft
4	Theodore Roosevelt	25	Jimmy Carter
5	Harry Truman	26	Calvin Coolidge
6	John Kennedy	27	Richard Nixon
7	Thomas Jefferson	28	James Garfield
8	Dwight Eisenhower	29	Zachary Taylor
9	Woodrow Wilson	30	Benjamin Harrison
10	Ronald Reagan	31	Martin Van Buren
11	Lyndon Johnson	32	Chester Arthur
12	James Polk	33	Rutherford Hayes
13	Andrew Jackson	34	Herbert Hoover
14	James Monroe	35	John Tyler
15	Bill Clinton	36	George W. Bush
16	William McKinley	37	Millard Fillmore
17	John Adams	38	Warren Harding
18	George H. W. Bush	39	William Harrison
19	John Quincy Adams	40	Franklin Pearce
20	James Madison	41	Andrew Johnson
21	Grover Cleveland	42	James Buchanan

Note: respondents ranked the 42 presidents according to their success in international relations, relations with Congress, vision/setting an agenda, administrative skills, public persuasion, crisis leadership and moral authority.

Nixon did have an impressive understanding of international politics, and this showed itself most notably in the policies that he initiated towards the Soviet Union and Communist China, as well as in the Middle East. It was Nixon who began détente with the Soviet Union. It was Nixon who first opened up diplomatic relations with Communist China, even visiting Peking (Beijing) in 1972. And it was Nixon who began to woo Egypt away from its Arab neighbours in an attempt to find a solution to the difficulties over the creation of the state of Israel. Here's Nixon writing in an article in the prestigious and scholarly periodical *Foreign Affairs* as far back as October 1967:

> For the short run, this means a policy of firm restraint [with Communist China], of no reward, of a creative counter-pressure designed to persuade Peking that its interests can be served only by accepting the basic rules of international civility. For the long run, it means pulling China back into the world community — but as a great and progressing nation, not as an epicentre of world revolution.

Nixon wrote this just a year before Mao's Cultural Revolution swept through China. Many contemporaries would have been tempted to write off Nixon's views as at best misguided and at worst just plain wrong, but recent developments have shown that Nixon's understanding of China's future world role was extraordinarily accurate.

Jimmy Carter was a president who lacked this knowledge of international politics. He tended to run the USA's foreign policy according to how he thought the world ought to be, rather than how the world was. He made frequent miscalculations in his dealings with the Iranian government over the hostage crisis. Carter's foreign policy was often chaotic and contradictory.

In contrast, another one-term president, George H. W. Bush, had a consummate understanding of international politics. John Dumbrell, in *American Foreign Policy: Carter to Clinton* (1997), wrote:

> In many respects, George Bush was far and away the most successful foreign policy president of the post-Vietnam War period. Bush's personal diplomacy created and preserved the Gulf War coalition. The Cold War ended in apparent victory for America's liberal capitalist ideology. The Administration's refusal to 'dance on the Berlin Wall' [after it was pulled down] was magnanimous and salutary. Conceptual foundations had been laid for the New World Order, based on self-determination and multilateral cooperation against aggression.

Yet, for all his foreign accomplishments, Bush was defeated in 1992 in his re-election bid, having, in the minds of many Americans, spent too much time focusing on foreign adventures and not enough on the US economy. One election-year jibe at Bush was the bumper sticker that read: 'Saddam Hussein's still got a job. Have you?'

Moral authority

President Theodore 'Teddy' Roosevelt (1901–09) was in the habit of referring to the presidency as a 'bully pulpit', with the word 'bully' having the meaning of 'superb' or 'wonderful' and a 'pulpit' being that part of the church from which sermons are preached. Roosevelt therefore saw the office as a superb opportunity for 'preaching' to the American people — trying to persuade them to strive for higher ideals and to tread difficult paths. But, for presidents to succeed in the bully pulpit, they need moral authority, and by 'having moral authority' we mean being perceived by the majority of Americans as a person of integrity and therefore worthy of being taken notice of on matters of morality, both collective and individual.

In many modern administrations, the issue of moral authority — or, more usually, the lack of it — has been a subject of great significance. Presidents who are viewed as dishonest and lacking in candour and integrity suffer severe consequences. For Lyndon Johnson there was what became known as a 'credibility gap' over the progress of the Vietnam War. His successor, Richard Nixon, was famously reduced to pleading 'I'm not a crook' — but he was forced to resign his office and escaped the judgement of the federal courts only through a pardon given him by President Ford. Both Johnson's and Nixon's presidencies fell apart largely because of their perceived lack of moral authority, which was magnified at a time of war when the president was asking great sacrifice of his fellow citizens.

More recently, Bill Clinton's impeachment and trial on charges of perjury and obstruction deprived him of much of his moral authority. As happened during the Nixon debacle over Watergate, the President's loss of moral authority began to permeate other parts of US politics. Republican Senator Chuck Grassley of Iowa put it this way in an open letter to his constituents at the time of the President's trial:

> The President's actions are having a profound impact on our society. His misdeeds have caused many to mistrust elected officials. Cynicism is swelling among the grassroots. His breach of trust has eroded the public's faith in the office of the presidency. But the true tragedy in this case is the collapse of the President's moral authority. FDR once spoke of the presidency in this way. He said, 'The presidency is not merely an administrative office; it is pre-eminently a place of moral leadership.' Mr Clinton should note that.

Although Clinton was not a candidate for re-election, the question of his lack of moral authority and integrity was often raised during the 2000 election to decide whether he would be succeeded by Vice-President Gore or Governor George W. Bush. Here's Bush's vice-presidential running-mate speaking at that year's Republican National Convention:

> I have been in the company of leaders. I know what it takes. And I see in [George W. Bush] the qualities of mind and spirit our nation needs and our history demands. On the first hour of the first day [of his presidency] he will restore decency and integrity to the Oval Office.

The phrase about 'restoring decency and integrity to the Oval Office' was one that was often repeated by Bush himself during the campaign.

A president particularly needs moral authority at times of national crisis and disaster — President Reagan after the space shuttle *Challenger* exploded with the loss of all its crew; President Clinton after the Oklahoma City bombing; President Bush after 9/11. If the president is to raise the moral sights of the nation, it needs to be done from the moral high ground. In an article entitled 'This is no laughing matter', *The Economist* reported that when a short newsreel film was shown in a national chain of cinemas in USA, which included a shot of President Clinton putting his arms round a woman to comfort her after the Oklahoma City bombing, sniggering was clearly audible in most cinemas.

The World Trade Center on 9/11

An ability to persuade

The late Professor Richard Neustadt will always be remembered for his seminal work on the US presidency, *Presidential Power: The Politics of Leadership*, first published in 1960. It's a brilliant work, not only for its insight into the presidential office but also for the lucid and masterful way in which he explains his thesis. You can read Neustadt and not only learn about the presidency, but also learn how to write! Here is how the book's third chapter opens:

> In the early summer of 1952, before the heat of presidential campaign, President Truman used to contemplate the problems of the general-become-President should Eisenhower win the forthcoming election. 'He'll sit here,' Truman would remark (tapping his Oval Office desk for emphasis), 'and he'll say "Do this! Do that!" *And nothing will happen.* Poor Ike — it won't be a bit like the Army. He'll find it very frustrating.'

> Eisenhower evidently found it so. 'In the face of continuing dissidence and disunity, the President sometimes simply exploded with exasperation,' wrote Robert Donovan in comment on the early months of Eisenhower's first term. 'What was the use, he demanded to know, of his trying to lead the Republican Party?' And this reaction was not limited to the early months alone, or to his party only. 'The President still feels,'

an Eisenhower aide remarked to me in 1958, 'that when he's decided something, that *ought* to be the end of it, and when it bounces back undone or done wrong, he tends to react with shocked surprise.'

Truman knew whereof he spoke. With 'resignation' in the place of 'shocked surprise', the aide's description would have fitted Truman. The former senator may have been less shocked than the former general, but he was no less subjected to that painful and repetitive experience: 'Do this, do that, and nothing will happen.' Long before he came to talk of Eisenhower he had put his own experience in other words: 'I sit here all day trying to persuade people to do the things they ought to have sense enough to do without my persuading them. That's all the powers of the President amount to.'

In these words of a President, spoken on the job, one finds the essence of the problem now before us: 'powers' are no guarantee of power; clerkship is no guarantee of leadership. The President of the United States has an extraordinary range of formal powers, of authority in statute law and in the Constitution. Here is testimony that despite his 'powers' he does not obtain results by giving orders — or not, at any rate, merely by giving orders. He also has extraordinary status. Here is testimony that despite his status he does not get action without argument. Presidential power is the power to persuade.

'Presidential power is the power to persuade.' That's quite right — and every holder of the office ignores that fact at their peril. Where the UK prime minister can wield real power, the US president must usually persuade: the prime minister commands; the president influences.

Take George W. Bush's 2003 tax cuts as an example. That year Bush had proposed a $726 billion tax cut to Congress, one in which his Republicans had a majority in both houses, but the President still had to persuade. With the tax cut debate in full swing on Capitol Hill, the President headed out of Washington on a tour of targeted states to rally support for his proposals. He made a bee-line for those states in which Republican politicians were proving recalcitrant in supporting his tax-cutting package — states like Ohio. On 23 April, the President was in North Canton, Ohio, as the following *Washington Times* story reported:

> President Bush swooped on Thursday into the home state of a fellow Republican who refuses to go along with his drive for more than half a trillion dollars in new tax cuts. Bush used his ninth trip to politically strategic Ohio to lean on Senator George Voinovich, a Republican from that state who has refused to support his tax reduction plan. 'It's important that Washington respond to some of the problems we face,' Bush said on the shop floor of a ball-bearing factory in this northeast Ohio city. 'For the sake of the country, for the sake of the workers of America, Congress needs to pass this jobs growth package soon.'

A popular president appealing directly to people over the heads of other Washington politicians can be a powerfully persuasive pitch. Senator Voinovich claimed on this occasion that he wouldn't yield to this persuasion by the President.

Six days after his Ohio visit, the President invited Republican congressional leaders for a meeting at the White House. He called a meeting with House Speaker Dennis Hastert and Senate Majority Leader Bill Frist to urge them to push for the biggest tax cut possible. Two days later, Frist was back at the White House again, this time accompanied by other key Senate Republicans and Federal Reserve Chairman Alan Greenspan.

On 9 May, the House voted 222–203 for a $550 billion tax cut. Although the tax cut figure was well below the President's starting figure, Bush hailed it as a victory. A week later, there was another 'victory' for the President as the Senate voted 51–49 for a $350 billion tax cut. At one point, it looked as if Vice-President Dick Cheney might be needed to break a 50–50 tie in the President's favour. The outcome was assured, however, when one wavering Republican senator agreed to support the deal on the morning of the vote. And that was Senator George Voinovich of Ohio. Presidential persuasion can win votes.

The President's job wasn't finished yet. There was still the hurdle of conference committee to be jumped. As the conferees met in late May, the President made a rare visit to Capitol Hill to endorse a Republican deal of a $350 billion tax cut. The conference committee's $350 billion tax cut package eventually passed the House by 231–200 and the Senate by 51–50 with the Vice-President casting the tie-breaking vote.

Clearly, there is a link between persuasive skills and skills of communication. Ronald Reagan was dubbed 'the great communicator', but political commentator David Broder always thought this title wasn't quite right and later wrote:

> The reason that Reagan was persuasive was that he had first persuaded himself of the truth of his utterances. When someone hung the title of 'The Great Communicator' on Reagan, I thought to myself, 'It should be "The Great Persuader"'.

Presidents need to work hard even for limited successes. But to maximise their chances of success, presidents need to bargain, compromise and persuade. This is how Cronin and Genovese see the president's role:

> The politics of shared power necessitates the development of agreement between a president and Congress. The model, or theory of government, on which the American system was founded is based on consensus and coalition building. Consensus means agreement about ends; coalitions are the means by which the ends are achieved. Since power is fragmented and dispersed, something (crisis) or someone (usually a president) has to pull the disparate parts of the system together.

> A consensus can be formed if the president has a clear, focused agenda; if the president can forcefully and compellingly communicate a vision; and if the public is ready to embrace that vision. If a president can develop a consensus he can then muster the power to form the coalitions necessary to bring the vision to fruition.

Simply placing a legislative package at the doorstep of Congress is not enough. Presidents must work to build support within and outside Congress. High skill levels may give a president greater leverage to win in the congressional process. Skills such as knowledge of the congressional process, good timing, bargaining, deal-making, persuasion and coalition-building skill; moving the public; setting the agenda; self-dramatisation; arm-twisting; trading; consultation and co-optation, and even threats can all be used to advance the president's goals.

Conclusions

With such a daunting list of factors required for presidential success, it may not be surprising that so few presidents are rated 'great'. The reality of the presidency is, according to James Pfiffner (*The Modern Presidency*, 1994), that it is 'not a powerful office'. Pfiffner concludes that, as a result, 'presidents cannot command obedience to their wishes but must persuade others that their best interests lie with presidential preferences'.

David Mervin (*The President of the United States*, 1993) seems even more pessimistic about the likelihood of presidential success. 'Given the plethora of potential obstacles that stand in their way, it sometimes seems almost miraculous that presidents accomplish anything at all of significance, especially in domestic policy,' he writes. Cronin and Genovese see the presidency as an office of 'high expectations yet limited power; many demands, yet few resources'. Most presidents discover that 'opportunities to check [their] power abound', while 'opportunities to exercise [their] power are limited'. Indeed, Cronin and Genovese seem mystified by what exactly might lead to a successful and effective presidency:

Novelist Somerset Maugham once said, 'There are three rules for writing a novel. Unfortunately, nobody knows what they are.' We are tempted to conclude that there are three rules to being an effective president, yet no-one knows exactly what they are.

Task 7.1

Read Source A and answer the questions that follow.

Source A

All presidents want to be successful, but what does it mean to be a success? High popularity? A good historical reputation? Achieving one's policy goals? A high congressional support score? Getting one's way?

If success is measured merely by getting one's way, then many bullies are successful. But success in leadership means more than getting what one wants.

Task 7.1 (continued)

In determining success, we must always ask, 'power for what ends?' because power divorced from purpose is potentially dangerous and democratically undesirable.

In a democracy, people tend to get the government they deserve. If we look upon government as the enemy and politics as a dirty word, our anger turns to apathy, allowing power (but not responsibility) to slip through our hands; we look at politics not as a means to achieve public good, but as a necessary evil; we see elections as the choice between the lesser of two evils or the evil of two lessers; we presume that our democratic responsibilities are satisfied merely by the act of voting every so often; or we drop out of politics. In short, if we abandon politics, power abandons us.

In a democracy, a successful leader pursues and uses power, not for selfish ends, not to aggrandise his or her own status, but to achieve the goals of empowerment. Democratic leaders are educators, they are visionaries. They move the government in pursuit of the consensus generated from the values of the nation. They appeal to the best in citizens and attempt to lead the nation towards its better self.

Michael Genovese, *The Power of the American Presidency, 1789–2000* (2001)

(a) Why, according to Genovese, can presidential success not be measured merely by how often the president 'gets his own way'?

(b) What does Genovese suggest as the criteria for a successful president?

(c) Choose a modern-day president (since the 1960s) whom you think best illustrates the criteria of a successful president. Give reasons for your choice.

(d) Choose a modern-day president who you think did not illustrate these criteria. Give reasons for your choice.

Guidance

(a) The key to this question is in the second paragraph of the extract.

(b) The key to this question is in the final paragraph of the extract. To get some ideas, you might consult the C-SPAN survey of presidential leadership in Table 7.2 on page 102. To look at the survey itself, go to **www.c-span.org/PresidentialSurvey/**

Further reading

- Cronin, T. E. and Genovese, M. A. (2004) *The Paradoxes of the American Presidency*, Oxford University Press.
- Healy, G. (2008) *The Cult of the Presidency*, Cato Institute.
- Mervin, D. (1993) *The President of the United States*, Harvester-Wheatsheaf.
- Pfiffner, J. (2005) *The Modern Presidency*, Thomson Wadsworth.